LEAVING CERTIFICATE

LESS STRESS
MORE
SUCCESS

GW00578114

Art History
Revision

Áine Ní Chárthaigh

Gill & Macmillan

Gill & Macmillan
Hume Avenue
Park West
Dublin 12
with associated companies throughout the world
www.gillmacmillan.ie

978 07171 47007

Design by Liz White Designs
Artwork by Keith Barrett
Print origination by Carole Lynch

The paper used in this book is made from the wood pulp of managed forests.
For every tree felled, at least one tree is planted, thereby renewing natural resources.

For permission to reproduce photographs, the author and publisher gratefully acknowledge
the following:
© akg-images: 92T, 109T, 194B; © Alamy: 18B, 21, 55, 63BL, 64TR, 65TL, 65BR, 73, 76, 79,
91T, 91B, 92B, 98, 101, 102, 103, 104, 105, 106, 107T, 107B, 109B, 110C, 110B, 200; ©
Bridgeman: 54TR, 54CL, 54BR, 56T, 56B, 61, 71, 92V, 111T, 111B, 113TL, 113TR, 113B,
114, 117T, 117B, 118, 119, 120T, 120C, 120B, 121, 122, 124T, 124B, 125T, 127, 128, 129,
130, 131, 134T, 134B, 135, 137, 139T, 139B, 142T, 142B, 144, 145T, 145B, 146T, 147, 148T,
155T, 155B, 157T, 157B, 160, 162, 163T, 163BL, 163BR, 165, 166T, 166C, 166B, 167, 169,
170, 171, 173T, 173B, 176T, 176B, 179T, 182T, 182C, 182B, 183, 198, 199; © Department of
Environment, Heritage and Local Government: 20, 43T, 48, 52T, 63BLL, 63BR, 64TL, 64CL,
64CR, 64BL, 64BR, 65TR, 65BL, 69, 72, 77, 78T; © Getty Images: 19, 63BC, 74, 88, 100,
110T, 125B, 136, 140, 148T; © Mary Evans: 179B; © National Gallery of Ireland: 146B; ©
National Museum of Ireland: 23, 27T, 27C, 27B, 28C, 28B, 29T, 29C, 29B, 30T, 30C, 34, 35T,
35C, 36, 37, 38, 42T, 42TC, 42C, 42B, 45, 46, 47, 58T, 58B, 59, 60T, 60C, 60BL, 60BR, 62,
63TL, 63TR; © Photolibrary: 78B, 80; © Statens Museum for Kunst: 194T; Courtesy of Aidan
O'Sullivan: 18T, 52C, 52B.

CONTENTS

Leaving Certificate Art

Art is a very pleasant and satisfying Leaving Certificate subject to study. It does, however, pose a particular challenge to students, because both **practical and written work** must be prepared to a very high standard in order to achieve a high grade. This requires hard work and concentration. Exam time is particularly busy and you must **prepare** thoroughly so that you can display your artistic skills to the full. You also need to **research** the given topics on the examination papers.

If you are looking for a high grade in Leaving Certificate Art, be encouraged that **Art is like any other exam**. Take the time to analyse the content of the course. Then work out a personal strategy and apply it. Don't worry about 'talent': 90 per cent of the course is hard work! **So if you are prepared and you work hard, you will do well.**

key point

Art presents real challenges because of the nature and content of the work. Both practical and written areas are broken into several components, and to achieve a high grade you must do well in all of them.

Exam format

PAPER	EXAM DURATION (HOURS)	TIME OF YEAR	MARKS ALLOWED
Imaginative Composition or Still Life	2 ½	May	100
Design or Craftwork	2 ½	May	100
	5	May	100
Life Sketching	1	May	50
History and Appreciation of Art (3 essays, each worth 50 marks)	2 ½	June	150

Imaginative composition or still life

Painting or drawing from imagination.

or

Painting or drawing a group of objects.

Students receive a paper with suggested starting points three weeks before the exam.

Design or craftwork

Design: This is offered as a choice with Craftwork. A well-worked sketch is required for one of the crafts chosen from a list.

Craftwork: This is offered as a choice with Design. A well-worked sketch and a piece of craftwork must be fully executed on the day within the exam time.

Students prepare beforehand and bring their sketches with them.

Life sketching

Drawing from the human figure.

A standing pose is completed in 15 minutes and a longer pose in 35 minutes.

Students must draw the full figure and it may be completed in any medium.

History and Appreciation of Art

The fields of special study covered by the exam are as follows:

- **Section I**: Art in Ireland (from prehistoric times to the present).
- **Section II**: European Art (from AD 1000 to the present).
- **Section III**: General Appreciation topics based on everyday visual experience.

The History and Appreciation of Art paper offers a choice of topics and will include one from each special study area. You will be asked for three full, illustrated, essay-style answers, one from each of the three sections of the paper. Each essay carries equal marks.

History and Appreciation of Art

The Art syllabus was set in 1970 and has never been revised. History and Appreciation of Art was designed to cover a very comprehensive area, but examination of this material was intended to be very general. Over the years the style and content of the exam paper has changed. **Questions on current exam papers are framed to test detailed knowledge of specific study areas.** Section III: General Appreciation offers students an opportunity to discuss general visual topics, but even in this section the questions can be quite specific.

key point

The exam paper has determined the syllabus for some time now. So, study past exam questions from the previous five or six years very carefully. Always check the marking scheme. This will help you to study in a more focused way.

Preparing for the History and Appreciation of Art exam paper

You should:

- Study specific sections only.
- Study each of these three chosen sections in as much detail as possible.
- Carefully examine past papers and marking schemes.
- Practise answering questions from past papers.

- Use the internet, libraries and other sources for coloured images and extra information.
- Visit museums and galleries whenever possible so that you can see the original works.

The exam paper normally offers good choice. In recent years at least one question can be guaranteed for each area.

Study Areas

Choose your study area from the following:

Section I: Art in Ireland

Study **one** area in detail and have outline knowledge of another.

1. Pre-Christian Ireland
- The Stone Age.
- The Bronze Age: early, middle and late.
- The Iron Age/Celtic/La Tène era.

2. Early Christian Ireland
- Architecture.
- Manuscripts.
- Metalwork.
- Stone carving/High Crosses.

3. Georgian Ireland
- Palladian architecture and decorative arts.
- Neoclassical architecture and decorative arts.

Section II: European Art

Choose **one** area only to study in detail.

4. Medieval Europe
- Romanesque architecture and sculpture.
- Gothic architecture and sculpture.
- Gothic stained glass.
- Fourteenth-century Gothic architecture.
- Fourteenth-century Gothic painting and sculpture.
- Painting in Italy: Giotto.

5. The Renaissance
- Painting: early and high.
- Sculpture: early and high.
- Architecture.
- Renaissance in Venice.
- Renaissance in northern Europe.

6. Impressionism and twentieth-century art movements

- Painting in nineteenth-century France.
- Sculpture in nineteenth-century France.
- Modern European art movements.
- Individual artists associated with nineteenth- and twentieth-century art movements.

Section III: General Appreciation

Topics vary considerably, but there are usually questions on the paper that fit the topics listed below. Some of these topics can be studied (e.g. film and design). Others depend more on a general awareness of visual surroundings.

- Museum and gallery visits.
- Film studies.
- Local public sculpture.
- The built environment.
- Graphic design, interior design and product design.
- General topics relating to visual appreciation.

Below are some tips that could help you in your revision:

- Learn your chosen sections thoroughly.
- Make a revision plan of key points.
- Examine previous exam questions.
- Use your own words to describe artefacts and works of art.
- Apply the knowledge gained in practical art classes to your discussion of works of art.
- Make written comparisons of earlier and later examples, wherever relevant.
- Study questions on previous exam papers.
- Examine marking schemes from previous years.
- Read the Chief Examiner's report.

Writing an essay

Structuring your essay

Before writing your essay, make a plan of your points, then:

- Introduce the subject with some general information relating to historical background or to the topic.
- Make a point and expand on it. Then move on to the next point and expand on that.
- Make comparisons, where relevant.
- Include quality sketches as you go.
- Label your sketches and include points of information.

Introduction

The introduction to your essay should include brief points of background information that will be developed throughout your essay.

- Point 1: information and historically correct facts. Named illustration 1.
- Point 2: information and facts. Named illustration 2.
- Point 3: information, facts and opinion. Named illustration 3.
- Point 4: information, facts and opinion. Named illustration 4.
- Concluding sentence: personal opinion.

Writing style

This is up to you. The important element is the information you can provide, so you can choose different writing styles. Options include:

- Traditional-style essay in which points are developed in paragraphs with an introduction and conclusion. Use the essay writing skills you have developed for Leaving Certificate English.
- A series of bullet points of varying lengths.
- A combination of bullet points and paragraphs.
- Use of different colours for headings.
- Use of a coloured sketch as your introduction.

Make your essay special!
Textbooks are designed to give you the facts only. Your essay should be individual and should reflect your reactions to the artworks. It should be written in a special and colourful language — yours!

Sketches

- Each exam answer must be illustrated. Remember: 10 marks are allotted for sketches/diagrams in each question.
- Sketches should analyse the work of art or make a visual point.
- Each sketch must be labelled and notes should be added.
- Marks are allocated on the amount of information the sketch conveys to the examiner.

Writing an individual essay

Instead of simply rewriting dry passages from a textbook, give your essay a personality of its own. Here's how:

- Try to see the artworks firsthand in situ or in galleries. This is bound to enrich your response.
- Use sources like the Internet or library books to look at images in colour. Take as much time as you can to absorb these wonderful works of art, which have stood the test of time.
- Read about the artworks and the artists who made them. Imagine what the artists were thinking; appreciate their efforts.
- Now tell your reader! Include the facts, of course, but make your essay really interesting.
- Describe what you see with enthusiasm and mean it. Let your response come from the heart. Use words that are meaningful to you alongside the visually descriptive language you have learned in class or from your textbook.

Compare and contrast

- It is really important to compare and contrast the work of artists, and to compare and contrast one artwork with similar examples. It shows that you have a wide knowledge base and it will make your points stronger.
- Make sure to study several artists and artworks from a period — not just the most popular.

Discuss

- When a question makes a statement, always discuss that statement fully. It is not enough to say 'I agree with the statement' and simply carry on.
- The statement should form the basis of your complete essay, but you must include your own opinions based on solid facts from your studies.

Sample questions and answers

- Throughout this book there are sample essays written by students. Use them to help you write your own essays.
- Each sample essay is an example of an appropriate response to a question, but it is by no means the 'right' answer. There are so many ways to respond to any given question. Your answer should reflect your individual response to a question.
- Remember also that some answers are much better written in point form with headings and paragraphs.

Exam time

Breakdown of marks

- Leaving Certificate Art is marked out of a total of 400 marks. The History and Appreciation of Art paper carries 150 marks, so it accounts for 37.5% of your overall grade in Art.
- Answer three questions on the paper.
- Choose one question only from each section, i.e. one question from Section I, one question from Section II and one question from Section III.
- Each question carries 50 marks.
- Each question is marked in the following way: 40 marks for written answer, 10 marks for sketches.

Time management

- The time allowed for the exam is 2 ½ hours.
- Since each question carries equal marks, it is essential that you divide your time equally between the questions.
- Work out a time plan that allows you enough time for writing and sketching.
- Stick to your time plan, so that you don't end up rushing the last question.
- Use a watch in the exam, so that you can keep an eye on time!

Suggested time plan for the exam paper

- Take **5 minutes** at the start to read the complete section of the paper relevant to your studies. In these 5 minutes, make sure you:
  - Carefully select the questions you are going to answer.
  - Pay special attention to questions with colour illustrations.
  - Look carefully at the choice of category question in Section II: European Art.
  - Read Section III: General Appreciation carefully. Don't automatically opt for a question on museum, exhibition or gallery visits: there might be a general question that suits you.
- Spend 48 minutes on your chosen question from Section I. Use these 48 minutes as follows:
  - Take 1 minute to read the question. Read it carefully; pause; then read it again to make sure you understand it completely.
  - Spend 35 minutes on your written answer.
  - Spend 10 minutes on accompanying sketches.
  - You are left with just over 2 minutes to spare!
- Repeat this 48-minute time plan for your chosen questions from Section II and Section III.
- If you manage to keep any spare time for the end of the exam, use it to polish up sketches or tidy up loose ends in your written answers.

Length of essays

- Students frequently ask how long each essay should be. As a rough guide, you should write 2½ pages of A4 paper and you should accompany this with one sketch.
- If you attempt to write or draw more than this for each essay, you are likely to run out of time.
- However, these are guidelines only and there are many variable factors. The amount of pages you use for each essay will depend on: the size of your writing; the speed at which you can write; and whether you use points or paragraphs.
- Whatever the length of your essays, make sure that you address all parts of the question asked.

Body of the essay

It is essential that you:

- Focus on the clues given in the question and then select only the relevant facts and information.
- Avoid using memorised set pieces. These may not be relevant and might lead you off the point. Remember: no marks can be given for irrelevant information.
- Write as if your examiner has never heard of anything related to the artwork you are discussing. Never assume that your reader knows what you are talking about.
- Always give general background information relevant to the period or style in your answer. This is absolutely essential to convey your grasp of the artistic achievements.
- Describe and discuss some of the important characteristics of the era and its place in history. However, this need not be too long or detailed.
- Provide two or more specific detailed examples of artists and their work for each answer.
- Break up written text with paragraphs, underlined headings and spaces.
- Attempt an answer in all three sections: never leave one out! You will pick up at least some marks for an attempt. Remember: losing an entire 50 marks is equal to not turning up for the Life Drawing exam.
- Sketches are important:
  - Make drawings that clarify your points in a visual way.
  - Label and use tone or colour if appropriate.
  - Add notes to draw attention to particular points.
  - Frame with neatly ruled lines.

exam focus

The colour illustration is a good one to choose if it suits. A good description of the given picture with personal interpretation will gain you a lot of marks before you even start.

Using the colour Ilustration

When answering a question with a colour illustration given on the accompanying sheet, keep the following points in mind:

- Always refer to the illustration itself and make sure that it forms the basis for the answer. Marks are specifically allocated to this.
- Information relating to the art history of the period in question is very important, but in this question you must focus on describing and discussing the given picture.
- Focus on examining the visual, creative and aesthetic aspects of the illustration.
- Discuss art elements like composition, colour and techniques and use language appropriate to art in your essay.
- Even if the picture is previously unknown and not in the textbook, it is important to remember that the illustration itself is a test of general visual awareness and ability to interpret an image. You can draw on the skills you have gained in the wider history and appreciation course.

Choosing from a category: Section II (usually question 13, 14 or 15)

 Answer (a), (b) and (c).

(a) Choose a work that fits into one of the following categories:
- A painting or graphic work featuring water.
- A painting depicting a battle or war.
- An equestrian painting or sculpture.
- A Baroque or Rococo palace.
- A painting by an Expressionist artist.
- A nineteenth-century poster.
- A sculpture by Auguste Rodin (1840–1917).
- A Modernist or Post-Modernist building.
- An installation or video-based work.

(b) Describe and discuss the work you have chosen and give your opinion on why you consider it to be a good example of its category. Refer to the artist's style and technique.

(c) You should also include a brief reference to at least one other example from the same category or at least one other work by the painter/sculptor designer/architect you have chosen. Use sketches to illustrate your answer.

- Read the above question very carefully, as it often offers an alternative to specific questions and sometimes gives you scope to write on a special topic of your own choice.

- Take a moment to think of a suitable work and artist you may have studied in your own chosen area.
- Questions vary from year to year, so read the requirements of this particular question very carefully before attempting to answer it.
- Ask yourself if this is a good example of the category.
- Justify your choice before or in conjunction with your description of the work.
- Discuss the work itself, giving your own opinion.
- Refer briefly to information on the artist, but only as it is relevant to the chosen work.
- Refer to the artist's style and technique as part of your analysis of the work.
- Do not give a full account of the life and work of your chosen artist.
- Give another example from the list above or from the artist you have selected.

Marking scheme for the exam question on page 9

- Description/discussion of chosen work:
- artist's style
- technique
- media, etc.
  25 marks
- Why the chosen work fits the category
  5 marks
- Reference to other work by chosen painter/sculptor/designer/architect
  10 marks
- Sketches/diagrams
  10 marks

Total: 50 marks

Revision plans

WEEK	LESSON 1 (1 HOUR) SAT: 10AM–11AM • READ BOOK • RESEARCH INTERNET • MAKE NOTES • PLAN ESSAYS FROM EXAM PAPERS	LESSON 2 (30 MINS) TUES: 5PM–5.30PM • READ BOOK • READ OVER PREVIOUS ESSAYS AND HOMEWORK	LESSON 3 (30 MINS) THURS: 9PM–9.30PM • DRAW
WEEK 1 5 DEC	THE STONE AGE STONE MONUMENTS	BACKGROUND LIFESTYLE HOUSING	TOMBS PATTERNS ON STONES
WEEK 2 12 DEC	BRONZE AGE PERIODS ORNAMENTS METHODS OF DECORATION	BACKGROUND LIFESTYLE MINING ALLUVIAL	ORNAMENTS DECORATION
WEEK 3 19 DEC	LA TÈNE: THE CELTS & IRON AGE CULTURE LA TÈNE: ART MOTIFS	LA TÈNE ORNAMENTS	ORNAMENTS STONE DETAIL OF PATTERNS
WEEK 4 2 JAN	PUBLIC SCULPTURE AND THE BUILT ENVIRONMENT	READ OVER PAST APPRECIATION QUESTIONS	DIAGRAMS OBJECTS PAINTING SCULPTURE
WEEK 5 9 JAN	ROMANESQUE ARCHITECTURE CHARACTERISTICS	MEDIEVAL EUROPE THE CHURCH & SOCIETY PILGRIMAGES	ROMANESQUE VAULTS PLAN OF PILGRIMAGE CHURCH
WEEK 6 16 JAN	ROMANESQUE SCULPTURE TYMPANUM: AUTUN & VÉZELAY	ROMANESQUE ART THEMES & STYLE	SCULPTURE FROM AUTUN & VÉZELAY
WEEK 7 23 JAN	GOTHIC ARCHITECTURE CHARACTERISTICS COMPARISON TO ROMANESQUE	ORIGINS OF GOTHIC GOTHIC CATHEDRALS PURPOSE OF GOTHIC ART	RIB VAULTING FLYING BUTTRESS
WEEK 8 30 JAN	GOTHIC SCULPTURE SCULPTURE & ARCHITECTURE CHARTRES, REIMS, NOTRE DAME PARIS	COLUMN STATUES THE SAINTS IN ART	COLUMN STATUES FIGURES FROM THE DOORS
WEEK 9 6 FEB	STAINED GLASS FOURTEENTH-CENTURY SCULPTURE	CHARTRES CATHEDRAL SAINT CHAPELLE	THE BLUE VIRGIN OF CHARTRES
WEEK 10 13 FEB	PAINTING: INTER- NATIONAL STYLE	DUC DE BERRY WILTON DIPTYCH	WILTON DIPTYCH DUC DE BERRY

Work out your time per week and the material you need to cover. These sample plans may help you coming up to the Pre-Leaving Cert in early spring. Use a similar method to plan again for the exam in June.

State Examinations Commission website

Examination papers, markings schemes and a report from the Chief Examiner of Art are available at www.examinations.ie. To access examination papers, click on Examination Material Archive, then follow the links for type, year, examination and subject.

Chief Examiner's report

These reports are not released every year and may be several years old. However the information is still very useful and should inform your approach to answering as well as study. Included in the Chief Examiner's Report are statistics for the previous four years and an analysis of student responses to each of the questions. This information is a valuable study resource if it is used in conjunction with exam papers and marking schemes.

Internet links

Search the Internet for good illustrations and examples. Some websites relating to art history are excellent. The following is just a short list.

Pre-Christian Ireland

- www.megalithicireland.com
- www.shee-eire.com
- www.sacred-destinations.com/ireland

Early Christian Ireland

- http://en.wikipedia.org/wiki/Category:Celtic_art
- www.sacred-destinations.com/ireland

Georgian Ireland

- www.irish-architecture.com
- www.answers.com/topic/georgian-dublin

Medieval Europe: Romanesque and Gothic

- www.medart.pitt.edu
- www.sacred-destinations.com/france/sacred-sites
- www.wga.hu

Impressionism

- www.ibiblio.org/wm/paint/glo/impressionism

Appreciating art

- Always start your studies with Appreciation.
- What art are you making in school: painting, drawing, clay modelling, printing? Many artists have done this before you. Look at art; look the work of artists. It will make your own work far stronger.
- Visit a gallery if you can and spend time looking at the work. Enjoy it, write notes about it, and make drawings.
- Look around your locality. Is there public sculpture nearby? Find out who made it and when. What does it signify? Has the artist made other pieces nearby or in another part of the country? Discover why the artwork was placed there and who paid for it. Where did the materials come from?
- Visit your public library and do some research.
- Research your chosen artists and study areas on the internet.
- Seek out the best artwork. What artworks have stood the test of time?
- How well suited are your local architecture and environment? Be aware of the art in your locality. Are there posters on billboards? How effective are they?
- Seek out art in everyday objects. Is that magazine cover well designed?
- Look carefully at the Appreciation questions on recent exam papers. Try answering some that interest you.
- Now study the history of art–you are ready for it!

SECTION 1

Art in Ireland

Early Irish Art and Architecture – Chapter 2 and 3

- To develop a factual knowledge as well as a critical awareness of the artefacts, artistic styles and historical background of your chosen study area
- To explore the wide range of practical techniques used by artists of this time
- Acquire an understanding of how these works of art related to the function and materials used
- Be aware of outside influences on the development of early Irish art
- To identify the relationships between art and society

Architecture in Eighteenth-Century Georgian Ireland – Chapter 4

- To gain knowledge of the dominant Classical architectural style of the period
- To recognize and name the architectural and decorative features of the buildings
- To identify the functional and aesthetic qualities of the materials used in the exteriors and interiors
- To understand the concept of public buildings
- To identify the relationships between architecture and society
- To study original buildings
- Become familiar with appropriate terms

Stone Age or Megalithic Period (7000–2000 BC)

	Example	Form/ Structure	Decoration	Function
Portal tomb/dolmen	Poulnabrone, Co. Clare. Kilclooney, Co. Donegal. Brownshill, Co. Carlow.	Three to seven upright stones carrying one or two very heavy capstones that slope downwards towards the back.		Above-ground burial chambers.
Court cairn	Creevykeel, Co. Sligo.	A semicircular forecourt of upright stones leading to a gallery divided into separate chambers surrounded by an oval-shaped cairn or mound of stones.		Possibly used as burial places or as places of ritual or gathering.
Passage grave	Newgrange, Co. Meath. Dowth, Co. Meath. Knowth, Co. Meath. Located on a bend of the River Boyne.	Layout: Large tombs. Structure: Aboveground cross-shaped passage and chambers covered by a large man-made mound of earth and stones. The mound is surrounded by a circle of kerbstones and large standing stones. Building techniques: Corbel vaulting in the chambers. Large standing stones with cross beam roof stones on the passages.	Location: Entrance wall–white quartz stone. Decoration on the stones on the entrance, passage and roof. Technique: Pocking (carving/incision). Style: A range of abstract, geometric motifs consisting of circles, U-shaped arcs, parallel lines, sun-like shapes, spirals and ovals as well as triangles, zigzags, dots, chevrons and lozenges.	Burial chamber for cremated remains stored in decorated pottery urns. Possible place of worship.

	Example	Form/ Structure	Decoration	Function
Large mound 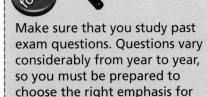	Knowth, Co. Meath.	Layout: Large mound surrounded by many satellite or small tombs. Two passages with separate entrances. The eastern passage is longer and ends in a cruciform shape. Both passages are lined with decoratively carved orthostats (standing stones).	Passages lined with decorated standing stones. Kerbstones decorated with spirals similar to those at Newgrange. Patterns based on diamonds and chevrons.	

Mesolithic Period or Middle Stone Age (7000–3700 BC)

- The first human settlers lived by hunting and gathering and settled mostly near riverbanks and lakes.
- Early housing consisted of animal skins spread over a bowl-shaped timber frame.
- Mount Sandel, Co. Derry is a mesolithic site discovered and excavated in the early 1970s. It provides evidence of how the early settlers lived and survived.

Neolithic Period or New Stone Age (3700–2000 BC)

- In the fourth millennium BC, the first Neolithic or New Stone Age farmers arrived in Ireland.
- They cleared forests using new tools, such as polished stone axes.
- The Céide Fields in north Co. Mayo is a Neolithic settlement believed to be about 5000 years old. It features stone field walls, houses and megalithic tombs preserved beneath peat.
- Porcellanite was the type of rock used by the new settlers to make axes and tools that chopped down large trees more easily.

> **exam focus**
>
> Make sure that you study past exam questions. Questions vary considerably from year to year, so you must be prepared to choose the right emphasis for the appropriate information.

- Peat bogs of Ireland: Land that was cleared of trees for agriculture suffered from erosion and evolved into peat bogs. A great deal of archaeological material was preserved beneath the bogs.
- Pottery, including ornamented cooking pots, was brought by the new settlers of the Neolithic period.
- Housing became more permanent with dwellings of circular and rectangular shapes.

- Changes to the landscape occurred because of tree clearing. By the end of the Neolithic period, communities were spread all over the island.
- There is evidence that people were in regular overseas contact.

Megalithic monuments

Stone burial monuments are evidence of strong spiritual beliefs in Neolithic people.

Megalithic tombs

These include:

- Portal dolmen.
- Court cairn.
- Passage tombs.

key point

Mega = Huge.
Lithos = Large stone.
Megalithic monuments = Great stone monuments.

key point

Learn by drawing!
Use drawing as a memory aid for each tomb and write notes around this.

Portal dolmens
Examples

- Poulnabrone in The Burren, Co. Clare.
- Kilclooney, near Ardara, Co. Donegal.

Design

- Two large standing stones and a lower back stone support a large roof stone positioned with its heavier end above the entrance.
- Single slabs rest against the side and back stones, forming the side chamber.

Poulnabrone Dolmen, Co. Clare

Court cairns
Example

- Creevykeel, Co. Sligo.

Design

- U-shaped or oval-shaped courtyard without a roof.
- Set in front of a covered gallery, which is the burial chamber and is divided into two or three by protruding stones like doorjambs.
- The cairn is usually a long triangular shape with the court occupying one end.

Court cairn at Creevykeel, Co. Sligo

Passage Tombs

Examples

- Newgrange.
- Knowth.
- Dowth.

Function

- Used as burial places; cremated remains were placed inside.
- May have been a place for ceremonies.
- Offered a focal point for communities.

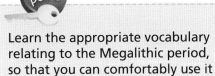

key point

Learn the appropriate vocabulary relating to the Megalithic period, so that you can comfortably use it in your essays.

Ornamented stones

- Abstract repeating patterns of circles and whirls.
- Patterns are likely to have an astronomical connection or relate to a form of calendar.
- Patterns may have had religious meaning.

Newgrange, Co. Meath

The passage grave at Newgrange, Co. Meath dates back to approximately 3000 BC.

Dimensions

- It is 85 m in diameter.
- The passage itself (including the chamber at the back) is 24 m in length, making it less than a third of the length of the whole mound.
- At its highest point inside the chamber it is 6 m tall.

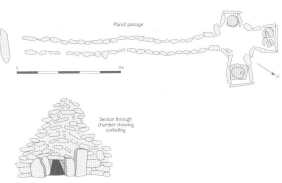

Plan of passage

Section through chamber showing corbelling

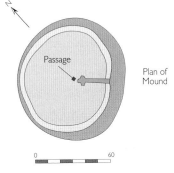

Passage

Plan of Mound

0   60

Plan of passage showing the cruciform shape of the chambers at the end

Newgrange, Co. Meath

Form

- A long passage ends in a chamber covered by a large mound or cairn of small rounded stones.
- It is surrounded by a kerb of massive slabs.
- It is surrounded outside by a circle of twelve tall monoliths or standing stones.

The Winter Solstice

- At sunrise on 21 December (the winter solstice) the light shines through a special roof box above the entrance.
- The light runs along the passage and the floor of the chamber. It is lit up for seventeen minutes.

The passage

- The long passage is lined on both sides with decorated standing stones known as 'orthostats'.

Corbelled roof

- The roof is corbelled: slabs are placed on top of each other so that each one partly overlaps the one beneath as they gradually rise in height.
- A large capstone rests on the centre.
- The outer edges of the corbels are sloped downwards to keep the interior dry.

Corbel vault section

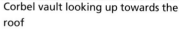

Corbel vault looking up towards the roof

Entrance stone

- The entrance stone is the most spectacular of the kerbstones.
- It has carvings of a triple spiral, double spirals, concentric semicircles and lozenges with a vertical line separating the circles.

key point

Tip for sketching the entrance stone at Newgrange

Draw the line in the centre. Next, draw the three spirals on the left and four on the right. Then fill in the lozenges.

Entrance stone and roof box.

Kerbstones

- There are 97 huge kerbstones surrounding the great mound.
- Kerbstone 52 is at the back of the mound and lines up directly with the entrance stone. The entrance stone and kerbstone 52 share many similar markings.

Kerbstone 52

Basin stones

- Large stones with a sunken centre are found in the chambers at Newgrange. These are called basin stones.
- It is likely that the basin stones were used to hold bones or cremated remains of the dead.

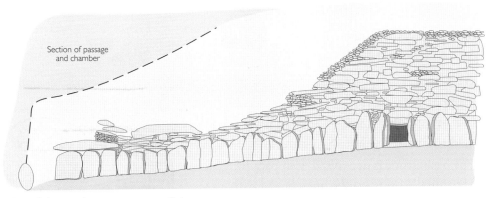

Section of passage and chamber

Section of the tomb at Newgrange. Light shines directly through the entrance box, allowing a narrower stream of light to project deep into the chamber.

Detail of pattern on the lintel above the roof box

Three-spiral pattern on the standing stone in the chamber at Newgrange

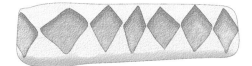

Patterned corbel stones in the roof of the chamber

Knowth

- Knowth is similar in size to Newgrange.
- Recent archaeology has uncovered the mound and 18 smaller satellite mounds.
- The art is really special at Knowth. It is reckoned that a quarter of Europe's Neolithic art is held here.
- Knowth remained a significant place of political and military power right up to Christian times.

Form

- A great mound with two passages opposite each other.
- The passages have separate entrances that do not connect.
- The eastern passage is longer and ends in a cruciform shape.
- Both passages are lined with decoratively carved orthostats.

Basin stone

- In a recess at the end of the eastern passage is a richly decorated granite basin stone.
- The basin stone is decorated with parallel horizontal scoring on the outside and with arcs and rays on the inside.
- Behind the basin stone is a large orthostat engraved with symbols.

Kerbstones

- There are 127 oblong kerbstones surrounding the great mound.
- The slabs were probably transported from several miles away.
- Angular and spiral inscriptions stop at ground level. This suggests that the stones were already in place before the art was applied.
- This impressive art suggests that the people were highly aware of astronomical function.
- Several kerbstones display symbolism that may be linked to the lunar calendar.

key point

In terms of archaeology, art, beauty and size, Knowth is far more impressive than Newgrange. It is reckoned that a quarter of Europe's Neolithic art is held here.

key point

An orthostat is a standing stone.

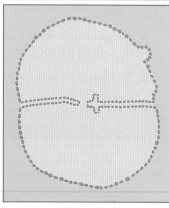

Ground plan of Knowth

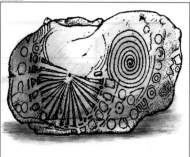

Engraved kerbstone at Knowth. Kerbstone 15 is possibly a sundial or lunar calendar.

Mace-head

- A decorative flint mace-head was found during archaeological excavations.
- It is carved in low relief style.
- The hole was probably for a wooden handle.

Woodhenge

- Near the eastern entrance is a circle of timber posts. This is called a 'woodhenge' and it was constructed between 2800 and 2500 BC.
- Archaeologists reconstructed the woodhenge using postholes to show how it would have looked.
- Evidence suggests it was used as an area for sacred rituals.

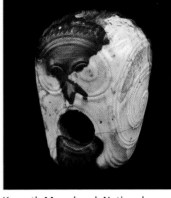

Knowth Mace-head, National Museum of Ireland

Dowth

- Dowth was built in the same period as Newgrange and Knowth and is similar to them in size.
- Considerable damage was done to Dowth when it was excavated in an unprofessional manner in 1847.

Below is a comparative study of questions on Newgrange from the 2004 and 2008 exam papers. The answers to both questions will be similar but will focus on different aspects. It is very important to be aware of this.

2004 Higher Level paper: Section I, Question 1

The Megalithic tombs in the Boyne Valley are evidence of a well-organised society in Ireland at the time they were constructed. Discuss this statement in relation to one tomb in particular, referring in your answer to its structure, decoration and function.

Illustrate your answer.

SAMPLE ANSWER

Newgrange is the finest example of a passage tomb. It was constructed around 3200 BC. It was built during the Neolithic Stone Age, when a farming community settled in the area. Located near the River Boyne in the Boyne Valley, Co. Meath, Newgrange is one of many passage tombs grouped together in the area. Together with the satellite tombs Knowth and Dowth, it is part of the cemetery known as 'Brú na Bóinne', which translates into 'Palace of the Boyne'.

Newgrange is a passage tomb, but it was also a place of spiritual importance to those who built it and it is evidence of how well-organised this society was.

Structure

After its discovery, but before excavations could begin, the mound collapsed. A loose circular cairn of stone covered the tomb and a kerb of massive slabs laid on their long edges with ends touching, surrounding the base of the cairn and forming a retaining feature. Outside this structure is 'the Great Circle' surrounding Newgrange. These tall, wide orthostats were erected after the construction of Newgrange. There were 35 stones in the circle, but only 12 remain today. No decorations are found on these stones. The mass of the cairn is composed of small water-rolled stones with layers of turf embedded to stabilize the pile. The builders of Newgrange must have possessed the skills of engineers and architects to have planned and built this great structure.

Archaeological discoveries

The entrance stone at the front is placed in line with kerbstone 52 at the back

Prof. Michael J. O'Kelly oversaw the reconstruction of Newgrange, which began in 1962. The outer wall of the tomb was decorated with white quartz taken from the Wicklow Mountains, interspersed with water-filled stones of granite. The people who built Newgrange originally must have used a log-and-pully system to move massive stones and build this structure. Newgrange, like many other passage tombs, sits on a hilltop. Knowth and Dowth are visible from Newgrange.

Skilled craftspeople

Kerbstone 52

Another skill that the people of Newgrange had was that of craftsmanship. There is much design work to be seen throughout Newgrange. A continuous circle of large slabs surrounds the base of the cairn. There are 97 in total but only 29 are exposed. Many of these slabs are decorated and two of the most interesting are the entrance stone and kerbstone 52. Some of these kerbstones are placed in sockets to maintain a continuous cairn. The skill of pocking can be seen on these stones as well as the art of banging out shapes in the stone using flint. The entrance stone, located to the front, is placed in line with kerbstone 52 (located directly at the back).

Decoration

These two kerbstones were decorated using flint and they display the abstract, non-representational, geometrical designs found throughout Newgrange. Designs such as spirals, lozenges, chevrons, cup shapes, concentric circles and the famous tri-circles are found within and outside the tomb. No natural representations of humans or animals are visible, but Newgrange is associated with some truly unique designs.

The triple circle design appears on a standing stone inside the chambers, facing the basin stones. This must have had some significance beyond the aesthetic. It may be a symbol representing birth, life and the afterlife. These carvings show that the builders had great artistic sensibility. The spiral could mean the sun. We can only guess today the true meaning of these decorated textures, but these designs must have carried some meaning for the Neolithic builders of Newgrange.

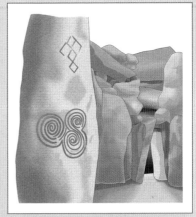

The triple-spiral design can be seen on a standing stone inside the chamber

The Winter Solstice

The lintel box, which faces southeast, is 2.4 m from the entrance. The carver would have marked out where the designs were going to be placed. They would have pocked out the lines or incised the designs, leaving parts in relief, as in the lintel above the entrance. Each year, on 21 December (the winter solstice) the

Corbel vault looking up towards the roof

sun shines through the roof box and lights up the passage. The builders had great understanding of the sun, knowing it where it shines when it rises at dawn.

The roof box of the chamber is corbelled: each stone partially overlaps the one beneath it and it moves in an inward direction. A capstone is placed on top to protect the chamber. This vault structure has remained intact for over 5000 years. The outer edges of the corbels are marked with water grooves for drainage. Water never enters the chamber and it has remained dry for 5000 years.

In the cell chambers lie four basin stones. Individual basin stones are made from granite that came from the Mourne Mountains. These stones contain remains of the dead. These stones were made smooth by rubbing one stone with another.

Function

We know that Newgrange was a burial ground, but it may have had other functions. It could have been an assembly place for the settled people. Ceremonies for worshipping the dead could have taken place there. The builders must have believed in the supernatural, since they built a sacred place for their dead. They left possessions with their dead and this suggests that they believed in an afterlife. The close connection with the winter solstice might mean that Newgrange was a site of celebration for a new year of farming or for worship of the sun.

The builders of Newgrange were intelligent, superstitious and incredibly skilled in many ways. They were artistic and creative; and they possessed engineering, architectural and organisational skills that enabled them to build and decorate an enormous structure riddled with motifs and still standing today.

2008 Higher Level paper: Section I, Question 1

Describe and discuss the stone carvings at Newgrange, referring to their location, motifs, and the techniques used;
and
Compare the carvings at Newgrange with one other example of stone carving from the pre-Christian period.

Illustrate your answer.

The following marking scheme applies to this question:

- Location of carvings: 10 marks.
- Discussion of motifs: 10 marks.
- Discussion of techniques: 5 marks.
- Discussion and comparison with other pre-Christian carvings: 15 marks.
- Sketches: 10 marks.
- Total: 50 marks.

Pattern on the Turoe Stone, Co. Galway

SAMPLE ANSWER

- *The introduction in this answer can be quite similar to the introduction in the answer to the 2004 question.*
- *The discussion of the stonework can be similar to the discussion of stonework in the 2004 answer.*
- *Below is a sample answer for Part 2 of the question:*

A total of 97 kerbstones surrounded the base of Newgrange. There are 37 of them visible now. Most of these stones are ornamental, especially the entrance stone and kerbstone 52. These kerbstones are slotted into sockets and act as a support for the mound. Kerbstone 52 and the entrance stone are decorated with geometrical, non-representational designs: cup shapes, lozenges, chevrons, spirals, the tri-circle, pocking incising. All of these are non-human and non-animal.

Turoe Stone

The Turoe Stone near Loughrea, Co. Galway is also an example of pre-Christian stone carving in Ireland. This stone from the Iron Age (500 BC–AD 500) is carved in a completely different style. The motifs show that it is carved in the La Tène style, named after the La Tène Celts from Lake Neuchâtel in Switzerland. These motifs are far less geometrical and show a representation of flowers. The artwork is much looser, with whirls of tendrils. It shows a Greek influence in its step pattern. The triskele in the Turoe Stone (three-legged trumpet) is more floral than the tri-circle patterns seen at Newgrange.

Bronze Age (2000–500 BC)

Beaker Pottery: Early Bronze Age (2000–1500 BC)				
Artefact	**Examples**	**Form**	**Decoration**	**Function**
Food vessels Burial urns Earthenware bowls Vases	Bowl-shaped food vessel (Aghnahily, Co. Laois). Vase-shaped food vessel (Topped Mountain, Co. Fermanagh). Vase urn (Priestdown, Co. Down). Encrusted urn (Newtown, Co. Limerick).	Small, squat, rounded bowls or taller V-shaped, narrow-based vases 10 cm to 20 cm high.	Incised patterns made with a comb. Slanted lines in a herringbone motif and cross-hatched triangles. Encrusted or applied relief strip lattice ornament.	Funerary vessels for cremated ashes or to accompany the dead in tombs.

Metalwork: Early Bronze Age (2000–1500 BC)					
Artefact	**Examples**	**Form**	**Decoration**	**Function**	**Metalwork Technique**
Discs	Pair of gold 'sun discs' (Tedavnet, Co. Monaghan).	Small discs of thin sheet gold 11.6 cm in diameter. Often found in pairs.	Cross motif of chevrons and zigzags. Repoussé technique.	Small holes near the centre suggest stitching to garments — possibly worn on the chest.	Circle cut from a thin beaten plate of gold. Decorated by hammering and punching.
Lunulae	Gold lunula (Ross, Co. Westmeath).	Crescent or half-moon shapes. 20 cm across.	Combinations of lines, zigzags and hatched triangles. Incision (cutting) technique.	Likely to have been worn as neck ornaments.	Shape cut from thin beaten sheets of gold with slightly thicker extensions at the ends for locking.

Metalwork: Middle Bronze Age (1500–1200 BC)					
Artefact	Examples	Form	Decoration	Function	Metalwork Technique
Earrings	Flanged gold earrings (Castlerea, Co. Roscommon).	Small, twisted rings with a 'collar' and rod-like ends. 3.6 cm in diameter.	Flanged and twisted.	Worn in the ears.	Four flanges created by hamming out the edges of an angled bar of gold. Twisted to 180°.

Metalwork: Late Bronze Age to Golden Age (1200–500 BC) Bishopsland Phase (1200–1000 BC, dated to the time of a hoard found in Bishopsland, Co. Kildare)					
Artefact	Examples	Form	Decoration	Function	Metalwork Technique
Twisted bands for waist, arm and neck	Gold Ribbon Torc (Belfast, Co. Antrim).	Gold twisted band with locking device. 17.5 cm in diameter.	Twisting.	Worn as a neck ornament.	Strap of gold beaten out from the centre to very thin edges before twisting. Thicker metal forms buttons at the end to interlock.
Bracelets	Gold armlets (Derrinaboy, Co. Offaly).	Curved broad bands of gold.	Broad ridges with smaller ridges. Repoussé technique	Worn as arm bands or bracelets.	Made from a length of broad gold ribbon. Thin edges of the ribbon coiled backwards and inwards to create a strong edge.

Metalwork: Late Bronze Age to Golden Age (1200–500 BC) Dowris Phase (900–500 BC, dated to the time of a hoard found in Dowris. Co. Offaly)					
Artefact	Examples	Form	Decoration	Function	Metalwork Technique
Dress fasteners	Gold dress fastener or fibula (Clones, Co. Monaghan)	Large, bow-shaped bar linking two concave bases or terminals. 21.5 cm long.	Engraved concentric circles on the terminals. Parallel bands and chevrons on the bases of the bow.	Garment fastener or double button (probably ceremonial).	Pure gold weighing over 1000 g. Concave terminals beaten to shape.
Gorgets	Gold gorget (Glenisheen, Co. Clare).	Curved sheet of gold with disc terminals. 31.4 cm in diameter.	Repoussé ridges with recessed rope moulding. Engraved concentric circles enclose a small conical boss on the terminal discs.	Neck ornament.	Semicircular band of beaten sheet gold with rolled edges. Terminal discs linked together by folded edges. A slit in the lower disc allows the band to slip through. Terminals stitched on with gold wire.
Lock rings	Gold hair lock rings (Gorteenreagh, Co. Clare).	Conical shapes with a slit at the side. 10 cm in diameter.	Concentric lines of tiny gold wires placed beside each other.	Likely to have been hair ornaments.	Made from four main pieces: a central split tube, two gapped conical plates and a circular binding strip.

Artefact	Examples	Form	Decoration	Function	Metalwork Technique
Bulla 	Gold-plated bulla (Bog of Allen, Co. Kildare).	Pendant-shaped 'bulla'. 6.4 cm long.	Concentric circles, semicircles, triangles and other patterns in repoussé.	Possibly worn around the neck as a pendant. May have served as an amulet or an object to ward off evil or ensure fertility.	Lead covered with sheet gold.
Leather, wood and bronze shields 	Bronze shield (Lough Gur, Co. Limerick).	Sheet bronze disc, 72 cm in diameter. A strap of bronze curved to form a handgrip is riveted to the back, 71.3 cm in diameter.	Ridges and rounded bosses. Large raised central boss. Repoussé technique.	Shield for use in combat against a slashing sword. Shields of wood and leather were more common in Ireland. Bronze is very rare.	Bronze thick enough to withstand a sword stroke would be too heavy, so to deflect the blow of the sword, six equally spaced concentric ridges were raised from the surface of a thin plate with six rings of raised bosses between.
Bronze cauldrons 	Bronze cauldron (Castlederg, Co. Tyrone).	Sheet bronze cooking pot with turned-out rim and handles, 56 cm in diameter.	Pointed rivets that hold the plates of sheet bronze together may also have collected heat to speed up the boiling process.	Cooking vessel for meat with two large rings to suspend it from a pole and carry it to a feast.	The rim is formed from the in-turned edge of the disc. Base formed by a dished bronze circular plate. Above this are three rounds of sheet bronze plates riveted together. Two pieces form the upper round. Handles are securely fastened to the rim with straps of bronze.

Settlers came to Ireland about 2000 BC and passed metalworking skills to the Neolithic people. The use of bronze brought significant changes to human activity because:

- It could be moulded into any required shape.
- It was a far stronger material than stone.

Everyday life in Bronze Age Ireland

The clearing of land and creation of bogland

- Metal axes made tree-cutting easier.
- A growth in population created pressure to find farmland. Forested areas of the lowlands were cleared.
- As the trees disappeared, the land became wetter.
- A thick blanket of peat was formed.

Preservation of objects in the bogs

- Large numbers of Bronze Age valuables have been found in the bogs of Ireland.
- They may have been deposited there as 'offerings' of one kind or another.

Housing

- Only very sparse evidence exists for housing and settlements dating back to the Bronze Age.

Cooking

- Examples of a Bronze Age cooking instrument known as a **fulacht fiadh** have been found in several parts of the country.
- The fulacht fiadh was a wood-lined trough in the ground, which was filled with water. A fire was used to heat stones and these were thrown into the water.

Fulacht Fia
Experiments have shown that water can be brought to boil in a fulacht fia in thirty minutes. If the water was kept at boiling point with hot stones, a leg of mutton wrapped in straw could be cooked in about four hours.

Bronze cauldrons

Large cauldrons were used for cooking. The bronze cauldron from Castlederg, Co. Tyrone is an excellent example of the technical brilliance achieved in sheet-bronze work.

Metalwork technique

- The metal sheets are fastened together by high-pointed rivets.
- Two heavy fittings, which hold the lifting handles, are securely attached to the rim.

Bronze cauldron, National Museum of Ireland

Function

- Used for cooking meat.
- Large rings allow the cauldron to be suspended from a pole and carried to a feast.

Burials

- Burials often took place in small Bronze Age tombs called cists.
- Cists were rectangular in shape.
- Bodies were placed in a crouched position and covered over with stone and earth.
- Tools, weapons and a small, bowl-shaped piece of pottery were often put with the person.
- This may indicate a belief in the afterlife.

The Beaker People

- Around 2000 BC, new settlers came to Ireland from Europe.
- Known as the 'Beaker people', they brought a new style of pottery in highly-decorated drinking vessels.

Stone circles

- Stone circles, stone rows, and standing stones are all dated to the Bronze Age.

Metalwork

Settlers brought the art of metallurgy to Ireland. People soon learned how to mine and process raw ores; craftsmen turned them into finished pieces.

Metals

- Gold, silver and copper were the first metals worked.

Copper

- The earlier part of the Bronze Age is sometimes referred to as the Copper Age.
- Copper was used in a pure state.

Bronze

- Bronze is an alloy of copper and tin.
- Copper was found in Ireland, but it is likely that tin was imported from Wales.
- Bronze was stronger than pure copper and led to more sophisticated weapons and tools.

Metal ores

Copper

- A Bronze Age mine was found at Mount Gabriel, Co. Cork.
- Copper was mined here.
  - t dates from 1500–1200 BC and has 25 mine shafts.

Silver

- Silver was mined in the Silvermine Mountains, Co. Tipperary.

Gold

- No gold mines have ever been found.
- It is assumed that **alluvial gold** was found in rivers and streams in the Wicklow Hills.

Tools, weapons and ornaments

Example

A bronze ceremonial shield from the Late Bronze Age was found at Lough Gur, Co. Limerick.

Form

- The shield found at Lough Gur shows a change in the style of combat in Ireland.
- A strap of bronze riveted to the back of the shield is curved to form a handgrip.

Metalwork technique

- Blows directed at the shield would have bounced off the ridges and rounded bosses, and reduced the force.

Function

- Probably for decorative purposes only, because it is too thin to be really effective.
- Wooden and leather shields of a similar design would have been used in real combat.

Gold ornaments

The National Museum of Ireland in Dublin has one of the largest and finest collections of Bronze Age gold ornaments in the world. Many spectacular pieces of gold jewellery have emerged over the years, particularly from boglands. The era has been called Ireland's first Golden Age.

Metalwork technique

- Metalwork from the Bronze Age has several distinct features.
- The same techniques were used on bronze and gold.
- Gold nuggets were beaten into thin sheets and cut into the required shape.
- Very thin strips were twisted to make fine wire.
- Straps of gold were hammered to make narrow bands, then twisted to make neck ornaments, earrings or girdles.

key point

Mount Gabriel is one of the few known Bronze Age mines. Archaeologists believe the walls were heated with fire and then splashed with water to shatter them. This made the process of extracting the metal ore easier.

key point

The word **alluvial** refers to anything that is deposited by flowing water, e.g. silt, sand, clay or gravel. Gold nuggets or dust found in this state are called alluvial gold.

key point

The best way to study these objects is to visit the National Museum of Ireland in Dublin. Alternatively, search for good illustrations in books or on the internet.

- Thicker bars were hammered at the edges and twisted to make neck ornaments called torcs.
- Casting techniques involved the pouring of molten bronze or gold.

Decoration

- Patterns of decoration were abstract and geometric.
- Repoussé technique was employed: a design was hammered on the reverse of a thin sheet of gold or bronze.
- Incision was used: cutting a design into the front.
- Compasses were used for decoration on circular objects.
- Twisting and flange twisting were also employed as decorating techniques.

Learn by making!
Cut out the objects in light card. Make incised decoration using a pointed instrument. Repoussé using a ballpoint pen on the reverse. Colour them in gold and paste them into your sketchbook.

The Bronze Age has three distinct periods:

- Early (2000–1500 BC).
- Middle (1500–1200 BC).
- Late (1200–500 BC).

Early Bronze Age ornaments (2000–1500 BC)

Gold discs

Form

- Thin gold discs.

Function

- Small holes near the centre suggest that these discs may be have been a kind of button that was once sewn onto a garment.

Metalwork technique

- Gold was beaten into a thin sheet using a hammer.
- Circles were cut from this and were decorated.

Gold disc, Early Bronze Age

Decoration

Repoussé in the form of a cross encircled by concentric bands of chevrons (zigzags) and dots.

lunula

d 1500 BC the repoussé method gave way to a new technique, that of incision or into the front of the object.

Example

- The lunula is a particularly Irish object.
- The National Museum of Ireland has 45 in its collection.

Form

- The word lunula means 'little moon' and refers to the crescent shape of the object.

Function

- The lunula is a neck ornament.

Gold lunula, Early Bronze Age

Metalwork technique

- Gold was beaten into a thin sheet using a hammer and then cut into the crescent shape.
- The paddle-shaped ends are slightly thicker so that they can be turned to form a clasp.

Decoration

- The decoration is incised on the front, but the plate is so thin that the designs can be seen clearly from the back.
- The front is plain except for parallel lines around the edges and several bands at the pointed ends.
- Decorated with triangles and chevron strokes.

Middle Bronze Age ornaments (1500–1200 BC)

The period from 1200 BC onwards was a very prolific time for gold ornaments.

Examples

Earrings, armlets, anklets, waist-bands and torcs or neck ornaments.

Metalwork technique

- Ribbon twisting, bar twisting and flange twisting.

Flanged gold torc, Late Bronze Age

Flange twisting

- Thicker or triangular-shaped bars of gold were flattened at the edges to form a thin flange before twisting.

Flanged gold earrings

Form

- Small rounded earrings.

Flanged gold earrings, Middle Bronze Age

Metalwork technique

- A V-shaped groove was cut on each face of a small rectangular bar of gold and the edges were hammered out to form four flanges before twisting.

key point

Small gold earrings are copies of a type found in Mediterranean areas, which were made by soldering two pieces of gold together before twisting. Irish goldsmiths did not yet know the technique of soldering, so they used their own methods.

Late Bronze Age ornaments (1200–500 BC)

The late Bronze Age is famous for its huge quantity, quality and variety of gold ornaments.

- Craftsmanship had reached a very high level of sophistication.
- Goldwork produced in Ireland during the late Bronze Age is of the highest standard known in Europe.

Gold ribbon torc from Belfast

Form

- A strap of gold was beaten to reduce its thickness progressively from the centre out towards the edges.
- The ribbon was then twisted.
- The narrow ends were worked into rounded knobs to form an intricate locking device.

Function

- Torcs were neck ornaments.

The Gleninsheen Gorget

Gorgets are unique to Ireland. The National Museum of Ireland has quite a number in its possession.

Example

- The Gleninsheen Gorget, which was found in a rock crevice in the Burren, Co. Clare

Form

- A crescent-shaped sheet of gold with a gold disc at each end.

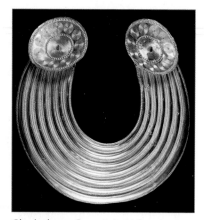

Gleninsheen Gorget, Late Bronze Age

Function

- Possibly used as neck ornament for ceremonial purposes.
- May also have been worn on the chest.

...work technique

...ade from a thin sheet of gold with a narrow strip rolled and pressed around the ...v edge.

- The terminal discs consist of two circular plates, one larger than the other.
- To attach the collar, the edge is inserted into a slit on the under disc and is sewn in place with gold wire. The smaller of the discs is placed on top and the edges of the disc underneath rolled over to finish the raw edges.

Decoration

- Decorated all over with raised ridges and rope moulding in repoussé.
- The discs are covered with patterns of concentric circles and repoussé-raised bosses.

Gold hair rings

Form

- Two cones are held together with a circular binding strip and tube designed with small bosses on the inside for gripping the hair.

Function

- Considered to be used for holding hair in place.

Metalwork technique

- The grooves on the surface of the cone are made with wires closely bound together and finely soldered.

Gold dress fastener

Gold dress fasteners (fibula) are the Irish version of a northern European model, which was probably worn on the chest to fasten two sides of a garment together.

Example

The Clones Dress Fastener

Form

- A connecting bow, decorated at the base with small hatched triangles, joins two hollow, cone-shaped terminals.

Gold Dress Fastener

Function

- Dress fasteners are like double buttons that would fit into buttonholes.
- Likely to have been worn for ceremonial purposes.

Decoration

- Both terminals are decorated with a series of small concentric circles surrounding a central dot.

Sleeve fasteners

Sleeve fasteners were similar in design to dress fasteners, but were smaller in size.

Metalwork technique

- These were cast in one piece and terminals hammered into the required shape afterwards.

Gold bulla

Form

- A small locket.

Decoration

- Lead covered in gold foil and decorated with repoussé designs of concentric circles, semicircles, triangles and other patterns.
- These patterns may form a human face.

Function

- May have been an amulet: a charm worn to ward off evil or to promote fertility. Probably worn about the neck on a chain, like a locket.

Gold Bulla

The end of the Bronze Age

The limits of the Irish Bronze Age are difficult to state precisely, but it is generally accepted to have died away around 500 BC when people from Europe associated with the superior Iron Age culture arrived in Ireland. These people are more popularly known as the Celts.

Below is a comparative study of questions on The Bronze Age from the 2005 and 2008 exam papers. The information required for each answer is similar, but a slightly different emphasis should be placed on each one.

2005 Higher Level paper: Section I, Question 1

Name, describe and discuss three gold objects from the Bronze Age in Ireland, making specific reference to their function, form and the types of decoration used; **and**
Describe the techniques used in their production.
Illustrate your answer.

SAMPLE ANSWER

The discovery of metal was a key event in human history. It was the first material ⌐____ could be moulded into any shape and was stronger and more useful than ____⌐. The first metal widely used was bronze–an alloy of copper and tin. This ____common throughout Europe around 4000 BC but it took another 2000 years ____ for settlers from France to bring this knowledge to Ireland.

These new settlers were known also as the 'Beaker people', named after the shape of the pottery they made. They produced a considerable amount of pottery and the shapes were quite complex and most were ornately decorated. As the bronze-working Beaker people settled, their culture blended with that of the Neolithic Irish and the Irish Bronze Age began.

The Bronze Age is divided into Early Bronze Age (2000 BC–1500 BC) and Late Bronze Age (1200 BC–500 BC). Bronze was used to make jewellery and weaponry. The copper was mined in Mount Gabriel, West Cork. To extract this mineral, they would heat the walls of the mine, splash cold water onto them and pound out the ore while the wall was cracked. Tin was imported from Cornwall, England. Gold was widely used and alluvial gold (found in the riverbeds) came from the Wicklow Mountains and was possibly obtained through trade also.

Decoration

New methods such as repoussé (hammering out a design from the back) and twisting/flanging were used to decorate artefacts in both gold and bronze at this time.

Examples

Sun discs

Gold ornaments known as 'sun discs' date from this period. Sun discs are always found in pairs. The best example of these was found in Tedavnet, Co. Monaghan. A circle was cut out from a sheet of beaten gold. The decoration was hammered out in repoussé and two small holes were created in the centre of the cross-like motif. A possible explanation as to the function of these objects was that they were large buttons stitched to garments, with thread or wire fitted through the holes.

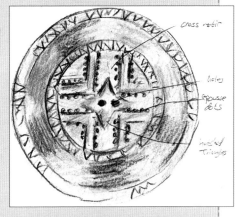

Gorgets

Another gold ornament is the 'gorget'. This neck collar is unique to Ireland and the National Museum of Ireland has several in its collection. One of the finest is the magnificent Gleninsheen Gorget, so called because it was found in a rock crevice in Gleninsheen, Co. Clare. The semicircular section is connected to two terminal discs. The discs themselves have repoussé dots and incised concentric circles. Incising means the design was cut into the front rather than the back. These discs are connected by a gold wire that is stitched to the semicircle's lower half. The lower half is cut from gold and has repoussé rope mouldings along it. This ornament is far too heavy to be worn as everyday jewellery, so it might have functioned as a neck ornament for ceremonies or rituals.

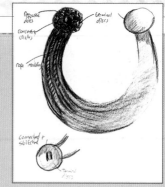

Earrings

Other examples of gold ornaments are the torc earrings found in Castlerea, Co. Roscommon. These earrings consist of a straight piece of gold, twisted at 180°. They functioned in the same way as modern-day earrings and are just one of many examples of torcs that have been found. Another example is the ribbon necklace found in Belfast.

The Gold Bulla

My final example of a gold ornament is the bulla found in the Bog of Allen, Co. Kildare. These badge-like artefacts might have been attached to a weapon or some other object for decorative purposes. This object is made up of layers; a layer of gold covers the lead underneath. This tiny ornament is beautifully decorated and carries abstract ornamentation.

Designs found on Bronze Age ornaments could be used today by designers of modern jewellery. The concentric circles, hatched triangles, parallel lines, chevrons and dots are all non-human and non-representational. The geometric designs are very aesthetic on the shimmering gold (e.g. the gold gorget) and even the basic designs could be incorporated with fashion.

2008 Higher Level paper: Section I, Question 2

Irish Bronze Age gold artefacts reflect both the design skills and craft skills of their makers.

Discuss this statement with reference to the form, function, decoration and metalworking techniques of any two named gold objects from this period;

and

Write a brief account of the Bronze Age people in Ireland and on their sourcing of raw materials for their gold artefacts.

Illustrate your answer.

key point

When you are asked to discuss a statement, it is extremely important that you do so.

SAMPLE ANSWER

- *Open with your discussion and expand on detailed description and information later.*

Some of the finest and most beautifully crafted gold ornaments and jewellery were produced in Ireland during the Bronze Age (2000 BC–500 BC). The beauty of these artefacts and the care taken in their making would suggest that gold was a symbol of power and wealth at that time and that they were made for people of high status in those early communities.

Skills

The quality of the design and the impressive range of skills available to metalworkers of this time can be seen in the wonderful collection in the National Museum of Ireland in Dublin. Techniques used in the production of ornaments included: hammering out paper-thin sheets of gold; moulded shapes; as well as the twisting and flanging of long strands. Decorating techniques involved 'incision' or cutting designs onto the face of the object; and 'repoussé', which involved pushing out a raised design from the back of the object. One of the most striking gold ornaments comes from the Early Bronze Age. This is the lunula–a crescent-shaped collar made from a thin sheet of gold. The National Museum of Ireland has several on display. The design of this object and its decoration is particularly impressive.

More intricate and different types of ornaments were made during the Late Bronze Age, including torcs (neck ornaments of twisted gold), dress and sleeve fasteners and waist-bands. One of the most unique is the gorget–a large neck ornament found only in Ireland. The National Museum has quite a number of these. Interestingly, they were all found around the area of the Shannon in the west of Ireland.

The design of these splendid objects is also extremely impressive...

- *Continue with a detailed description and sketch of the gorget.*
- *Move on to more general information on the Bronze Age in Ireland, as in the previous essay.*
- *The second part of the question will require a brief account of the sourcing of raw materials, as given in the previous essay.*

Iron Age and La Tène (1200 BC–AD 15)

	Metalwork: 500 BC–AD 100				
Artefact	Examples	Form	Decoration	Function	Metalwork Technique
Torcs, collars and neck rings	Gold torc, 19.4 cm in diameter, found at Broighter, Co. Derry in a hoard containing a gold model of a boat with oars, and other ornaments.	Two conjoined half hoops with a decorative fastener.	Two interlocking curves of repoussé foliage trumpets and spiral bosses. Plain surfaces covered in compass-incised fine lines.	Neck ornament.	Decorated flat, gold plates rolled around a form and soldered. Tubes then filled with hot resin and bent into hoops.
Trumpets, discs, swords and scabbards	Bronze trumpet from Lougnashade, Co. Armagh, 186.5 cm long.	Very long tubular curved trumpet with a rimmed circular bronze disc at the mouth.	Disc decorated with curvilinear spirals, wiry curves, tendrils and bosses in high relief. Repoussé technique.	Musical instrument.	Tube made by rolling edges of a sheet of bronze and riveting them to an interior strip.
Bronze crown	Petrie Crown, (named after antiquarian George Petrie), 15 cm high.	Fragment. Circular discs mounted on a band of bronze. Conical horns rise from behind discs.	Curvilinear low-relief patterns produced by cutting away the metal. Enamel bosses on the discs. Oval curves and ornamental birdheads on the horns.	Possibly a crown. Small perforations on the hoops suggest stitching to fabric.	The base is riveted to the band, which is brazed to the discs. A folded sheet of bronze forms the shape of the horns with the edges riveted to an under sheet of copper.

Decorated stones			
Artefact	**Form**	**Decoration**	**Function**
Turoe Stone, Co. Galway	Domed granite boulder. Cut to shape. Approximately 1 m high.	Incised decoration. Step-like pattern around the middle. Upper body covered with curvilinear ornament of trumpet ends, triskeles and stylised animal heads.	Probably for use in ritual.
Castlestrange Stone, Co. Roscommon	Rounded boulder.	Swirls and spirals carved into the stone.	Probably for use in ritual.

At the end of the Bronze Age, Ireland came under the cultural influence of the European Celts. The Celts arrived in Britain and Ireland around 500 BC and within a few hundred years Ireland's Bronze Age culture had all but disappeared and Celtic culture had taken over across the entire island.

Art as evidence

- The Celts had not discovered writing, so they left no firsthand documentary sources.
- The main evidence of the influence of the Celts in Ireland is found in Celtic artwork.
- Objects with Celtic decoration were found mostly in the north and north-western parts of the country.

The word **Celts** comes from 'Keltoi', a term used by the Ancient Greeks to describe a large community or tribe of central Europeans. There are two distinct groups of Celts:

- **Hallstatt Celts** (1200–475 BC).
- **La Tène Celts** (500 BC to the first century AD).

Hallstatt Celts (1200–475 BC)

The Hallstatt Celts lived in the area around Hallstatt in central Austria. They became wealthy and influential through their control of the following crucial trade goods:

- **Copper** and **tin**, which were important for bronze.

- **Salt**, which was crucial for preservation of food.
- **Iron**, which gave them strong technological advantages.

Iron

- Iron was a far superior metal because it was stronger and more durable than bronze.
- It required much hotter fires to extract it from its ore, so working iron required considerable skill.
- Iron became very popular, but bronze continued in use also.

Wealth

- Richly-adorned tombs, assumed to be those of chieftains or royalty, were found in places associated with major Hallstatt cultural centres.

Art

- The Hallstatt style brought together several artistic traditions of European art styles.
- It was influenced by Greek and Italian art.
- Rigid geometric forms were most common.

La Tène Celts (500–15 BC)

- La Tène culture is named after the site near Lake Neuchâtel in Switzerland.
- La Tène people spread rapidly throughout Europe and occupied the lands that are now Switzerland, Belgium, Germany, the Netherlands, Brittany and Britain, before bringing their culture to Ireland.

Ceremonial offerings

- La Tène is one of the most important Celtic sites. It is believed that part of the culture involved throwing objects into lakes as a ceremonial offering.
- A huge quantity of exceptionally fine weapons and other objects were found in the lake at La Tène.

Irish La Tène Art

Influences

- La Tène culture had contacts far and wide throughout Europe.
- It was mainly influenced by Eastern and Greek foliage sources from the Mediterranean.
- It developed unique abstract compositions.

key point

La Tène developed unique abstract compositions of curvilinear patterns that flow over surfaces in themes of great vigour and originality.

Motifs and patterns

- Motifs in La Tène art are based on plant forms, e.g. honeysuckle and palm leaves with flowing leafy tendrils.
- Curvilinear patterns include waves, spirals and s-scrolls.

- An offshoot of the Waldalgesheim style reached Ireland. This style takes its name from a chieftain's grave near Bonn in Germany, where some highly ornate objects have been found.

Art as evidence of the Celts in Ireland
- Beautifully decorated metalwork found by archaeologists shows the spread of the La Tène culture in Europe from about 400 BC.
- Irish La Tène is unique in its style and it continued to develop long after European examples had become obsolete.

Metalwork technique
- The Celts brought skills such as soldering and enamelling and this was incorporated into Irish workmanship.

Metals used during the La Tène period in Ireland
- Iron was used for implements and weapons.
- Bronze continued to be used for practical as well as ornamental objects.
- Gold was used for ornamental objects.

Iron objects
- Very few items made of iron have survived. However, some very fine swords and scabbards have been found in various places in Ireland, mainly in Co. Antrim.

Bronze objects
A fine example of a bronze object from this period is the Loughnashade Trumpet.

The Loughnashade Trumpet
- It is likely that the Loughnashade Trumpet was s-shaped and played with the two parts bending in opposite directions.
- This splendid trumpet has a long, large, curved stem.
- It was found in Loughnashade, Co. Armagh.

The Loughnashade Trumpet

Form
- Two curved tubes of bronze with a joint in the middle form an elongated conical shape that opens to the trumpet mouth.

Function
- This Celtic trumpet was probably used as an instrument of war.

Decoration
- A rimmed circular disc at the trumpet mouth is decorated with high-relief repoussé curvilinear designs.

Metalwork technique

- A sheet of bronze was rolled to make the tube.
- This was riveted to a strip of metal on the inside.

The Petrie Crown

This little object is named after George Petrie, a famous collector in the nineteenth century.

Petrie Crown, La Tène Period

Form

- Circular, concave-shaped discs are mounted on a band of metal with conical horns behind.
- A row of small holes on the band suggests that fabric may have been stitched to it.

Function

- It is considered to be a crown and was possibly worn on special occasions.

Decoration

- All the pieces are decorated in low-relief curvilinear patterns, which is cut away rather than repoussé.
- Stylised bird heads feature at the end of the spirals and trumpet curves. Those on the sweeping curves of the horns are particularly beautiful.
- The discs have individual patterns: there is a setting for a bead on one, and a stud of red enamel in the central boss of the other.

Metalwork technique

- The horns were made by folding a sheet of bronze into a conical shape and riveting the edges to an under sheet of copper.
- The design continues over the rivets, indicating that it was cut away after the horn was in position.

Gold objects

The Broighter Hoard

A hoard found at Broighter, Co. Derry is the richest collection of gold objects from Iron Age Ireland. Unfortunately, when the hoard was discovered by farmers ploughing a field, some damage was caused to the items. The hoard consisted of:

- A little boat with oars and a mast.
- A bowl.
- Two chain necklaces.
- Two twisted necklaces.
- A collar (torc).

The Broighter Collar

Form

- This beautiful gold torc is most elaborately made.
- It was broken in two pieces and the piece that may have been a decorative hinge at the nape of the neck is missing.

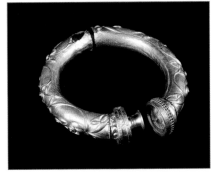

The Broighter Collar

Function

- Neck ornament.

Decoration

- The repoussé decoration is based on foliage and leaf motifs.
- Raised spiral bosses have been clipped on to give the appearance of flower heads.
- The plain spaces at both sides of this are decorated with fine compass-drawn lines.
- This combines older, traditional methods of decoration with the newer, more decorative La Tène style.

Metalworking techniques

- The decoration was applied to the sheets of gold while they were flat.
- These were then rolled into tubes, soldered together and filled with hot wax to heat the metal before bending.
- It is made in two half-hoops, with a decorative fastener.
- An elaborate locking device was attached to the front end of each hoop.

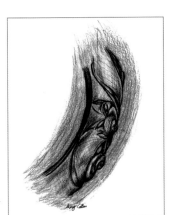

Detail of the ornament on the Broighter Collar

Decorated stones

A large number of carved stones were created in the late Iron Age in Ireland. It is not known what purpose they served, but it was probably for some kind of ritual. The complex, swirling patterns on these are similar to those found on central European Celtic culture ornament.

Examples

- The Turoe Stone, Co. Galway.
- The Castlestrange Stone, Co. Roscommon.

The Turoe Stone

- The stone was moved to its present location on the lawn in front of Turoe House, Co. Galway in the mid-nineteenth century. Before that, it stood for centuries at a *lios* (fairy fort) some distance away.

- Some historians believe it was carved in France and brought to Ireland in Celtic times before being moved further west.
- Its size and weight and the fact it is carved from local stone suggest that it was carved on the spot.

The Turoe Stone

Form

- A large, rounded stone pillar.

Function

- Various theories have been applied to the stone but none can be proven.

Decoration

- The surface is rounded and smoothed.
- The background is carefully chiselled away to produce the low-relief decoration.
- Decoration consists of leafy curvilinear designs.
- Spirals, circles and curves in undulating whirls cover the stone completely.
- A single triskele (a three-legged motif of trumpet curves) appears in the centre of one of the panels.
- A band of geometric patterns similar to a Greek step-pattern encircles the base.

Expanded drawing of the ornament on the Turoe Stone, showing that while the pattern is all over the stone, it is planned to have four distinct sides.

Castlestrange Stone

- The Castlestrange Stone is located at Castlestrange House, near Athleague, Co. Roscommon.

Decoration

- A continuous swirling pattern.
- This is engraved, rather than carved in relief like the Turoe Stone.

Ogham Stones

- Irish was written for the first time using the Ogham script made up of groups of strokes set in lines or angles.
- Pillar stones or boulders displaying Ogham are found mostly along the south coast of Ireland.

Figures and heads

- Some representations of Celtic gods have been found in Ireland.
- These are mostly made of stone, although wooden examples have also been found.
- Stone heads with a number of faces were found throughout the Celtic world.

Examples in Ireland
- A finely carved head with three faces, in Corleck, Co. Cavan.
- Stone figure, Tandragee, Co. Armagh.
- Figures on Boa Island, Co. Fermanagh. The date of these figures is uncertain, but it is possible that they date back to the Iron Age.

The influence of Celtic Art

The influence of Celtic art lasted far longer in Ireland than the rest of Europe. Spirals, curvilinear motifs and other Celtic decoration were continued by artists and craftsmen during the Christian era. Celtic motifs can be found on some of the great treasures of Irish Art from the eighth and ninth centuries AD, over eight hundred years after the Iron Age.

2009 Higher Level paper: Section I, Question 1

The Iron Age in Ireland saw a change in the design and decoration of metal objects and stone carving. Discuss this statement making reference to one named example of metalwork and one named example of stone carving of the period;
and
Discuss briefly the influence of the La Tène style on later Irish art of the Early Christian period.

Use sketches to illustrate your answer.

The following marking scheme applies to this question:

- Discussion of statement with reference to the change in design and decoration in the Iron Age: 5 marks.
- Discussion of named metal work object: 15 marks.
- Discussion of named stone carving: 15 marks.
- Brief discussion of the influence of the La Tène style on later Irish art of the Early Christian period: 5 marks.
- Sketches: 10 marks.
- Total: 50 marks.

Websites

A great deal of information can be found regarding the monuments of the Boyne Valley on several websites. A series of articles on this website are particularly interesting: www.knowth.com.

There is plenty of interesting information at: www.ancientsites.com.

Images are particularly good at: www.mythicalireland.com.

Interesting bits and pieces can also be found at: www.shee-eire.com and www.megalithicireland.com.

It is always worthwhile to search online using key words, as new sites and articles related to archaeology may appear at any time!

3 Early Christian Ireland

Christianity in Ireland

- St Patrick came to Ireland in AD 432.
- This date traditionally marks Ireland's move to Christianity.
- Christianity in Ireland adapted and blended with Pre-Christian traditions.
- Roman influence also came to Ireland.

Early Christian Art in Ireland

- The establishment of Christianity in Ireland marks the beginning of a great period in Irish art.
- Christianity and Roman learning combined to create a dynamic force.
- Roman influence is found in the design of jewellery and manuscripts.

key point

St Patrick and other missionaries established small communities ruled by their own bishop; but in the two centuries that followed, there was a gradual shift towards monastic settlements. This made church organisation in Ireland very different from that of Britain or continental Europe.

Phases in Art in Early Christian Ireland

Phase 1: Fifth to eighth century

- Early monastic settlements.

Phase 2: Eighth and ninth centuries: the 'Golden Age' of Irish Art

- Manuscripts.
- Metalwork.
- Carved stone crosses.

Phase 3: Eleventh and twelfth centuries

- Revival of craftsmanship.
- Magnificent shrines for relics.

Architecture in Early Christian Ireland

Example	Location	Function	Date
Skellig Michael	Island off the coast of Co. Kerry.	Monastic settlement.	Sixth to eighth century.
Gallarus Oratory	Dingle Peninsula.	Place of worship.	Eighth or ninth century.
Round towers	Clonmacnoise, Co. Offaly. Glendalough, Co. Wicklow. Monasterboice, Co. Louth. Ardmore, Co. Waterford.	Storing valuables. Places of refuge.	Tenth century.

The 'Golden Age' of Irish Art

- Liturgical items were commissioned by the church: chalices, patens, Gospel books, carved crosses, croziers, bells and reliquaries.
- Objects commissioned by kings and aristocrats include jewellery, such as brooches.

Manuscripts: sixth to eighth Centuries

- Christianity brought literacy to Ireland and handwritten books were produced in the monasteries.
- These first Irish manuscripts are written in the distinctively Irish 'half-uncial' script.
- Irish missionaries travelled to England and Scotland in the sixth and early seventh centuries, bringing the new style of writing with them.
- Small books were written in the 'miniscule' script.
- Large manuscripts, illuminated in colour for use on the altar for special occasions, were written in the solemn, 'majuscule' script.

Manuscripts: seventh to ninth Centuries

- These were masterpieces of calligraphy and painting.
- They were more beautiful than anything in the rest of Europe.
- They were produced in a room called a scriptorium.
- Traditionally, they were kept in leather satchels that were hung on the walls.

Monasteries required considerable wealth for book production, because:

- A large herd of calves was needed for vellum (writing parchment made from calfskin).
- Expensive colours were often imported from abroad.
- Special books were elaborately bound and stored in ornate gold or silver boxes (shrines) encrusted with jewels and precious stones.

St Colmcille of Iona

- St Colmcille (also called St Columba) and his followers are particularly associated with manuscript production.
- St Colmcille established monasteries in Durrow, Co. Offaly and in Derry.
- In AD 563 he founded the monastery of Iona on a small island off the west coast of Scotland.
- The scriptorium at Iona is generally considered to have been the site of the production of the Book of Kells.
- The earliest surviving Irish manuscript, associated with St Colmcille, is called the Cathach of St Columba.

The Cathach: sixth century

- The Cathach is the oldest Irish illuminated manuscript and is dated to c. AD 600.
- 'Cathach' means 'battle book' and refers to a legend about St Colmcille.
- St Colmcille copied a valuable book lent to him by St Finnian and in one of the earliest disputes about copyright there was disagreement about ownership of this copy.
- The King of Tara ruled in a very famous judgment: 'To every cow her calf, so to every book its copy.'
- The dispute ended with a battle that claimed the lives of 3000 men.
- St Colmcille was exiled to Iona as a penance for this.

Decoration

- Black and white, with only a small amount of red and yellow.
- Confined to the first letter of each paragraph.
- The letters are surrounded by dots.
- Old Celtic motifs used in metalwork were adapted to be used in the book.
- Stylised animal ornament is a feature of the book.

Capital letters from
The Cathach

The Book of Durrow: late seventh century

- The Book of Durrow is considered to be the earliest decorated Gospel book.
- It is traditionally associated with the Columban monastery of Durrow.

Decoration

- The script is in the Irish majuscule hand with pages decorated in red, yellow, green and deep brown against a background of black or the plain vellum page.
- Some pages open with an ornamental capital letter.

The Lion in the Book of Durrow

Features

- The Book of Durrow is one of the first to have ornamental beasts.
- The decoration shows Germanic influence that made its way to Ireland from England.
- Before each gospel, there is a symbol of the evangelist as a stylised beast of Celtic ornament.

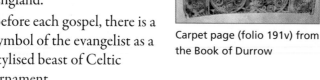

Carpet page (folio 191v) from the Book of Durrow

Carpet page (folio 192v) from the Book of Durrow

- There are large areas of undecorated spaces on many of the pages.

Carpet pages

- Elaborately ornamented pages called 'carpet pages' follow each of the evangelist pages. They contain:
- La Tène motifs, including spirals and triskeles.
- Animal ornament and interlaced beasts.

Function

- The Book of Durrow was probably intended for use on an altar, as it is too large to be carried around easily.

key point

A particularly violent Viking raid on the island of Iona in Scotland in AD 806 left 68 Columban monks dead. The others came to Ireland and took refuge in a new monastery at Kells, Co. Meath.

The Book of Kells: c. AD 800

- The Book of Kells is the most famous of all manuscripts.
- It contains the four gospels in the Irish majuscule script.
- There are 680 pages in the book and many are very elaborately decorated.

- The book may have commemorated the centenary of the death of Colmcille (AD 597).
- It was written at the beginning of the ninth century, around the time the monks left Iona to found the new Columban monastery of Kells. However, it is not known if the book was produced at Iona or Kells. Perhaps it was produced partially in each location.
- Compared with previous manuscripts, the Book of Kells has many new features, such as drawings of animals between the lines of text, new colours, and figurative scenes.

Colours

Five main colours are used in the Book of Kells:

- Red was made from red lead and it has kept its brightness very well.
- Yellow was made from egg-white and a mineral called orpiment. This colour has a shiny surface and looks like gold.
- Green was made from copper and it has an emerald colour.
- Purple probably came from a Mediterranean leaf and was imported into Ireland.
- Blue came from the precious stone called *lapis lazuli*.

key point

No gold was used in the Book of Kells, although gold leaf was commonly used in manuscripts of the time. Ultramarine blue was the most expensive colour, due to the scarcity of lapis lazuli, which is found only in the Himalayas.

Artists

The four main artists on the Book of Kells have been named as follows.

- **The Illustrator**: responsible for the Virgin and Child; the Arrest of Christ; and the Temptation.
- **The Portraitist**: responsible for the portraits of Christ, Matthew and John.
- **The Goldsmith**: responsible for the fine pages introducing the four gospels and the Chi-Rho page.
- **The Second Master**: responsible for the cats and kittens on the end of the Chi-Rho page and the charming depictions of animals and everyday life found in the margins and between the lines.

Decorated Pages

The Chi-Rho page

- The last and finest page of the book.
- Golden yellow is the most dominant colour.
- A large letter 'X' forms the central design.
- 'P' and 'I' are intertwined and end with a human head.

The Chi-Rho symbol

key point

The Chi-Rho symbol is a combination of the first two letters of the word 'Christ' in Greek: the Chi (CH) and the Rho (R). In Roman and medieval times, these two letters written together stood for Christianity.

- The letters are surrounded by very detailed abstract patterns of circles, spirals and triskeles.
- There are also tiny human and animal figures.
- Animal figures include: an otter with a fish in its mouth; cats with kittens; and a butterfly with spreading wings.

The Birth of Christ

- This is a Christmas page.
- Mary and Jesus are portrayed in a solemn, stylised manner.
- Four angels appear behind the main figures.
- The colours include several shades of purple and emerald green.
- Purple symbolises royalty.
- Six human figures represent the people that Christ came on earth to save.

Portrait of Christ

- Christ is seated on a throne. One hand is raised in blessing, the other is holding a book.
- He is coloured in red and purple.
- Above his head is a cross.
- Two peacocks symbolise everlasting life.
- Vine leaves and grapes grow from vases in which birds are standing.
- The birds have little white discs on their breasts, symbolising the Eucharist.
- Red, blue and yellow interlacing frames the picture.

The Arrest of Jesus

- Jesus is grabbed by two figures, but he looks calm and solemn, with arms outstretched in surrender.
- The figure is stylised and the folded red gown, face, hands and hair are all perfectly symmetrical.
- An arch overhead represents the Garden of Gethsemane.
- Two fierce monsters with tongues intertwined snarl at each other, suggesting violence and evil.

The Chi-Rho page from the Book of Kells

Birth of Christ page from the Book of Kells

Metalwork: eight to twelfth centuries

Artistic influences

Colmcille's monastery in Iona brought about links between Britain and Ireland. Anglo-Saxon artistic traditions were passed on to Irish artists and these blended with the earlier La Tène to form a unique style of art in Ireland.

- Solid silver was used for making objects like chalices.
- Enamel was used more frequently.
- A new glasswork technique called *millefiori* was adopted.
- New objects like large pins and penannular brooches for fastening garments became fashionable.
- Penannular brooches were so called because of the gap in the ring. They were developed from a Roman military-style brooch found in northern Britain.

Eighth-century metalworking techniques

- **Gold filigree**: Patterns made with delicately twisted gold threads.
- **Gilding and silvering**: Covering with a very thin layer of silver or gold.
- **Kerbschnitt**: Also called 'chip carving'; a method of casting that imitates wood carving.
- **Diestamping**: Shaping or cutting metal with a precision tool or die.
- **Enamel**: Glass crushed to a powder and placed in a mould before heating it to an extremely high temperature to make it liquid. It dries to a high-gloss finish.
- **Cloisonné**: A method of enamelling that separates the colours with thin strips of metal.
- **Millefiori**: Covering a cane of glass with layers of different coloured glass and cutting them into short lengths before setting into the metalwork. Motifs are similar to those found in manuscripts.

Metalwork: seventh and eighth century

The early eighth century is the era known as the 'Golden Age' and it is a time of perfection in Irish art.

Rinnegan Crucifixion Plaque

- Dates from the late seventh century.
- Found at Rinnegan, Co. Roscommon.

Form

- A small bronze plaque.
- One of the earliest examples of the crucifixion scene.

Function

- Numerous small holes suggest it was pinned to wood and was probably a book cover.

Decoration

- It was originally gilded (covered in a light film of gold).
- The figure of Christ resembles Christ on the stone cross at Carndonagh, Co. Donegal.
- The design is a combination of herringbone pattern, spirals and zigzags.
- The ornament on the garments is of the La Tène style.
- Surrounding Christ are smaller figures: angels, the lance bearer and the sponge bearer. The angels attending Christ have arms and legs, two pairs of wings and spiral designs at the points where the wings are attached.

St John's Crucifixion Plaque

Ardagh Chalice

- Dates from the eighth century.
- Found by a boy digging potatoes near Ardagh, Co. Limerick in 1868.

Form

- A moulded chalice with handles is joined to a base by a thick bronze stem.
- A cone-shaped foot gives it extra stability.

Ardagh Chalice

Metalworking techniques

- A wide range of materials and considerable technical skills were needed for its production.
- The bowl of the chalice is made of silver and the sumptuous decoration is offset by the plain areas of metal.

Decoration

- Interlace, animal interlace, scrolls, plaits and frets in gold wire filigree.
- Engraving, casting, enamelling and cloisonné.
- The chalice is surrounded by a band of gold filigree and red and blue glass studs.
- The names of all the apostles except Judas are engraved lightly into the silver under the band.
- The handles on both sides are decorated with coloured glass panels in red, blue, green and yellow. Between these panels are smaller panels of complex and skilled gold filigree work.
- In the centre of each side is a cross within a roundel. It is richly decorated with spirals of gold wire filigree work, coloured glass and a cloisonné enamelled stud in the centre.

- This flange has square blocks of blue glass separated by panels of interlace and geometric ornament.
- In the centre of the underside of the base is a circular crystal surrounded by gold filigree and green enamels.

Tara Brooch

- Dates from the eighth century.
- A penannular brooch. Pennanular brooches were based on a Roman design.
- Found on the seashore at Bettystown, Co. Meath. Nearby, a cliff had collapsed because of sea erosion. A jeweller who had the brooch for some time named it the 'Tara Brooch' and the name has remained.
- The Tara brooch is close in style to the Ardagh Chalice. It may have come from the same workshop.

Tara Brooch

Function

- Probably made for the personal adornment of a queen or king.

Form

- A ring brooch with no gap through which the pin can pass. This makes it a pseudo-penannular brooch.
- A chain and loops make up the fastening.
- The mesh chain suggests it may have been one of a pair originally joined together across the back of the shoulders.

Decoration

- The brooch is crowded with detailed decoration on the front and back.
- An astonishing amount of minutely detailed ornamentation fits into a very small space.
- Beasts made in raised gold thread curl and intertwine.
- On the back of the brooch are two plates with La Tène design, dark against a silver background.
- The chain is attached to the brooch by two animal heads.

Derrynaflan Hoard

- A hoard of liturgical items dating from the eighth century, including a chalice, a silver paten and a beautiful strainer-ladle.
- Found at the ancient monastery of Derrynaflan, Co. Tipperary.

Derrynaflan Chalice

- Closely related to the Ardagh Chalice, with similar decoration.

Decoration

- Filigree, enamelling, casting, engraving, stamping of thin gold and knitting of wire mesh.
- Cast glass studs, filigree gold animal interlace, engraving and knitted wire mesh surround the edges.

Derrynaflan Chalice

2006 Ordinary Level paper: Section I, Question 3

The Ardagh Chalice is shown here.

Answer (a), (b) and (c).

(a) What was its function?

(b) Describe the materials and techniques used to make and decorate it.

(c) Name and give a brief description of one other piece of metalwork from the same period.

Use sketches to illustrate your answer.

The following marking scheme applies to this question:

- Part (a): Chalice; hold wine at communion; store hosts; show wealth of the church: 10 marks.
- Part (b): Silver, gold filigree; glass studs; enameling; chip carving; spiral and interlace patterns: 4 x 5 marks = 20 marks.
- Tara Brooch or any penannular brooch; Derrynaflan; Crucifixion Plaque, etc. Description of item. 5 marks + 10 marks = 15 marks.
- Sketches: 5 marks.
- Total: 50 marks.

2009 Higher Level paper: Section I, Question 3

Name, describe and discuss in detail the two artefacts from the seventh and eighth century that are shown here.

In your answer make reference to the materials, decoration, form and function.

and

Explain briefly the techniques used in their production.

Use sketches to illustrate your answer.

The following marking scheme applies to this question:

- Name both artefacts illustrated on the accompanying sheet: 10 marks.
- Describe and discuss the Ardagh Chalice referring to materials, decoration, form and function: 15 marks.
- Describe and discuss the Tara Brooch, referring to materials, decoration, form and function: 15 marks.
- Brief explanation of techniques used in their production: 5 marks.
- Sketches: 5 marks.
- Total: 50 marks.

2006 Higher Level paper: Section I, Question 2

The decoration of the Book of Durrow displays evidence that it was influenced by the patterns and motifs found on stone and metal from the pre-Christian period.

Discuss this statement with reference to the photo shown here;

and

Describe and discuss one other page from any manuscript of your choice.

Illustrate your answer.

The following marking scheme applies to this question:

- Discussion of decoration of the Book of Durrow with reference to illustration: 15 marks.
- Stone: 10 marks.
- Metal: 10 marks.
- Describe and discuss one other page from another manuscript of choice: 10 marks.
- Sketches: 5 marks.
- Total: 50 marks.

Metalwork: eleventh and twelfth centuries

Artistic production in Ireland declined considerably during the late eighth and ninth centuries. However, the eleventh and twelfth centuries saw a great revival in craftsmanship. Stoneworkers and metalworkers produced works of art that equalled, if not outshone, the masterpieces of the earlier years.

Almost all the fine metalwork of this period is associated with the church and great care was taken in the creation and decoration of sacred objects like:

- Ornamented shrines for books.
- Reliquaries connected with relics of early Irish saints.
- Croziers.

Patrons

- The scale of production and the craftsmanship involved show that the arts were patronised by well-to-do clans and royalty of the time.

Scandinavian influence

- One of the most notable features of the metalwork is the blend of Scandinavian influences with native Irish work. This is seen particularly in the use of animal imagery.

Examples

- Shrine of St Lactin's Arm may have been made to hold the bones of a saint.
- Book-shrine of the Cathach.
- Shrine of St Patrick's Bell.
- Cross of Cong.
- Lismore Crozier.

Cross of Cong

- Turlough Mór O'Connor, King of Connaught, had a fragment of the True Cross. The Cross of Cong was the shrine made for this precious relic. It is one of Ireland's most important shrines.

Function

- A processional cross made to enshrine a fragment of the True Cross.
- The relic is protected by a crystal rock set in a silver mount and surrounded by gold filigree in the centre of the cross.

Cross of Cong

Decoration

- Tubular silver edging surrounds the curved outline of the cross.
- The cross surface is divided into ornamented sections of cast bronze thread-like snakes holding animal shapes.
- The staff and the cross are linked together by animal jaws biting the base of the cross.
- These animals have scaled heads, pointed ribbed snouts, little curved ears and blue glass eyes.

exam focus

Describe what you see
If the colour illustration features objects not so familiar to you, describe them from the illustration and draw on your knowledge of materials and metalworking techniques from other objects that are more familiar to you.

2007 Higher Level paper: Section I, Question 2

Describe and discuss the Derrynaflan Paten and the Lismore Crozier, which are shown here. In your answer make reference to their materials, form and decoration, and explain the techniques used in their production;

and

Explain and compare the function of these objects.

Illustrate your answer.

The following marking scheme applies to this question:

- Derrynaflan Paten (form, materials, decoration): 15 marks.
- Lismore Crozier (form, materials, decoration): 15 marks.
- Explanation of the techniques used in their production: 10 marks.
- Explanation and comparison of the function of the two objects: 5 marks.
- Sketches: 5 marks.
- Total: 50 marks.

Stone carving in Ireland

Pre-Christian				
Entrance stone, Newgrange, Co. Meath	Standing stones	Stone circles, Co. Kerry	Turoe Stone, Co. Galway	Castlestrange Stone, Co. Roscommon

Early Christian (Sixth to Eighth Century)

Reask Pillar, Co. Kerry

Aglish Pillar, Co. Kerry

Carved Crosses (Seventh Century)

Carndonagh Cross, Co. Donegal

Fahan Mura, Co. Donegal

High Crosses (Eighth Century)

Crosses at Ahenny, Co. Tipperary

North

South

Crosses of the Scriptures (Ninth Century)

Cross of Moone, Co. Kildare	Cross of Muireadach, Co. Louth

Eleventh and Twelfth-Century Crosses

Dysart O'Dea Cross, Co. Clare	Kilfenora Cross, Co. Clare

Stone carving in Pre-Christian times was done by cutting into stone slabs and standing stones. The tradition continued into early Christian times and Christian symbols began to appear along with the traditional ogham writing on standing stones. Legend has it that there was a fear in pre-Christian Ireland that carving the stone itself might interfere with the 'spirit' of the stone.

Stone carving in Ireland can be categorised as follows:

- Free-standing: seventh century.
- Ringed crosses: eighth century.
- Tall crosses of the scriptures: ninth and tenth centuries.

High Cross art

Made from sandstone, granite or limestone, the crosses feature several panels filled with carvings. Carvings can be abstract or figurative.

Abstract carvings

These comprise Celtic spiral or interlace designs:

- Zoomorphic (animal-shaped) motifs.
- Knotwork.

- Mazes.
- Labyrinths.
- Key patterns.

Figurative carvings

- Bible scenes from the Old and New Testaments.
- The crucifixion.
- Resurrection of Christ.

Characteristics of the Celtic High Crosses

The basic components of the Celtic cross are:

- Base.
- Shaft.
- Ring.
- Capstone.
- Sculpture panels.

Function of High Crosses

- It is not known exactly what function High Crosses served.
- They may have been boundary markers or monuments close to monasteries.
- Biblical scenes may have served as lessons.
- High Crosses have been called 'sermons in stone' because most people of the time could not read and might have used the High Crosses for spiritual learning.

Cross-inscribed stones

Grave slabs

Large numbers of engraved grave slabs are found near monasteries. They show cross designs and inscriptions.

Free-standing stones

- **Duvillaun Slab, Co. Mayo**: Greek cross with an early representation of the crucifixion.
- **Reask Pillar**, Co. Kerry: Carved Maltese cross with Celtic decoration.
- **Aglish Pillar**, Co.Kerry: Interesting combination of ogham and a Greek cross.

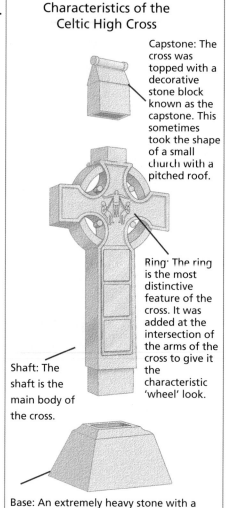

Characteristics of the Celtic High Cross

Capstone: The cross was topped with a decorative stone block known as the capstone. This sometimes took the shape of a small church with a pitched roof.

Ring: The ring is the most distinctive feature of the cross. It was added at the intersection of the arms of the cross to give it the characteristic 'wheel' look.

Shaft: The shaft is the main body of the cross.

Base: An extremely heavy stone with a socket forms the base and the cross is placed into this by means of a tenon.

Seventh-century crosses

Carndonagh Cross

- The first free-standing stone cross.
- The first to be cut in a cruciform shape.
- Decorated all over with broad ribbon interlace.
- On one side this is combined with figures.

Visit www.highcrosses.org for detailed pictures of a wide selection of Ireland's High Crosses.

Fahan Mura Slab

- Little shoulders in the place of arms.
- The only inscription in Greek seen in early Irish art.
- Decorated with broad ribbon interlace.

Eighth-century crosses: Crosses at Ahenny

- Two highly-ornamented crosses are found a few metres apart and at Ahenny, Co. Tipperary.

Form

- They are quite short with a widely spaced ring and wide base.
- A large portion of the shaft is above the ring.
- The north cross has an unusual conical-shaped cap.

Decoration

- Mainly abstract ornament, similar to metalwork of the time.
- Rounded bosses at the joints have no function in stone. This suggests that it might have been inspired by an object in metal.
- High-relief rope moulding is a distinctive feature around the edges of the ring and cross.

Crosses of the Scriptures: Ninth and tenth centuries

- Crosses of the Scriptures are decorated with panels of Bible stories that were popular lessons at the time.

Examples

- Cross of Moone, Co. Kildare.
- Muiredach's Cross, Monasterboice, Co. Louth.

Cross of Moone

Form

- Made of granite.
- Tall, slender, tapering and elegant in shape.
- The ring is quite narrow and the capstone is missing.
- The base is a tall rectangle with four even sides covered with carved figures.

Cross of Moone

Decoration

- The Cross of Moone was one of the earliest crosses to introduce biblical scenes.
- Panels depict scenes from the Old and New Testaments.
- The figures are square shaped and abstract.

Figurative Scenes

- Biblical scenes show how God intervenes to save the good from destruction.
- The west side of the base shows Daniel in the lion's den.

Visit www.sacred-destinations.com/ireland for excellent information and photos of Muiredach's Cross. Good pictures can also be found at www.bluffton.edu/~sullivanm/highcrosses/intro.html.

- The north side of the base shows the flight of the holy family into Egypt and the miracle of the loaves and fishes.
- The east side of the base shows the twelve apostles. This is probably the most famous scene on the cross. The square-bodied figures with large staring eyes fill the panel in three neat rows.

Muiredach's Cross

- This is one of the largest and best-preserved High Crosses. It gets its name from an inscription on the base.

Decoration

Muiredach's Cross

- All the carving is executed in bold rounded relief and is quite realistic.
- On the west façade, the central area within the ring depicts a crucifixion scene and below this three panels show scenes from Christ's life.
- The arrest of Christ is one of the scenes on the panels. In this scene, two figures grab Christ. He wears a cloak that is tied with a brooch similar to the Tara brooch. This denotes his royal status.
- On the base, two cats are carved in high relief. They sit in front of an inscription in Irish that translates: 'A prayer for Muiredach for whom the cross was made'.
- On the east façade is a depiction of the Last Judgment. The entire area is filled with a judgement scene that is extremely rich in detail. Interestingly, this depiction was carved about two hundred years before such scenes appeared in European Romanesque churches.
- Muiredach is thought to be an abbot who died in 922.

Twelfth-century crosses

- A completely different style of cross appeared around the twelfth century. These crosses show little or no stone carving.
- The ringed wheel-head was no longer a feature.
- A simple figure, usually Christ or a bishop, was placed in a prominent position on the upper part of the cross.

Example

- Dysart O'Dea Cross, Co. Clare

Dysart O'Dea Cross, Co. Clare

2009 Higher Level paper: Section I, Question 2

Describe and discuss the development of stone crosses in Ireland from the Fahan Mura Slab in Co. Donegal to the High Cross of Dysart O'Dea in Co. Clare. Give at least three specific examples and refer in your answer to form, imagery/decoration, stone working techniques and function.

Use sketches to illustrate your answer.

4 Architecture in Eighteenth-Century Georgian Ireland

The eighteenth century was a time of **peace and prosperity** in Ireland. A frenzy of building spread throughout the country as the wealthy ascendancy competed to construct elaborate town and country houses. Public buildings were the most beautiful the country had ever seen and craftsmen of all kinds came from Europe to work in Ireland.

key point

Eighteenth-century architecture is normally referred to as Georgian. It is named after four kings of England called George, who reigned in succession from 1714 until 1830.

exam focus

The amount of material needed for examination purposes can be studied without difficulty. If you are familiar with Dublin, this is a particularly good study area to choose for the exam.

Georgian Dublin

- Dublin is one of the finest Georgian cities in Europe.
- Dublin was very prosperous in the eighteenth century, with its own parliament largely controlled by the wealthy ascendancy.
- In 1800, the Act of Union abolished the Irish Parliament in Dublin.
- Dublin began to slide into decay and many fine Georgian houses were split up into tenements.

Georgian architecture

Architecture in the eighteenth century had high ideals. Aesthetic qualities of beauty, proportion and harmony were greatly sought after. The style was influenced by Classicism, which originated in Greece and Rome. This classical style became popular in England and later spread to Ireland.

key point

Take a tour
Many important Georgian buildings in or around Dublin are open to the public and some offer excellent and informative tours.

key point

In order to fully appreciate Georgian Dublin, you should visit the buildings. However, the book *Dublin: A Grand Tour* by Jacqueline O'Brien with Desmond Guinness is a beautiful publication. Everything you could want in information and pictures is here. Your local library should have a copy.

Classical orders

All classical architecture in the tradition of Greece and Rome is composed in a specific manner called an order. An order is an accepted way of assembling a column (supporting element) with an entablature (spanning element). This gives the architecture a particular character or 'order' of design.

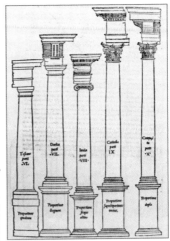

Classical orders of architecture

Eighteenth-century architectural styles

- **Palladian**: up to 1760.
- **Neoclassical**: dominant in the late eighteenth and early nineteenth centuries.

Prominent architects of the time

- Edward Lovett Pearce (1699–1733): An Irish architect.
- Richard Cassels (1690–1751): A German architect, who later changed his name to Richard Castle.
- William Chambers (1723–1796): A Scottish architect, who never visited Ireland.
- James Gandon (1743–1823): An English architect who trained in the office of William Chambers.

Palladian period: 1700–1760

Italian Influences

- Andrea Palladio was a sixteenth-century Italian architect.
- He wrote a book based on classical Roman remains.
- The book became the inspiration for a very fashionable style of architecture in England.
- 'Palladianism' first made its appearance in Ireland in large country houses in the eighteenth century.

Examples

Country Houses

- Castletown House, Co. Kildare.
- Russborough House, Co. Wicklow.
- Carton House, Co. Kildare.
- Westport House, Co. Mayo.
- Bellamont House, Co Cavan.

Public Buildings

- Parliament House (now Bank of Ireland, College Green, Dublin).
- Trinity College Dublin.
- Provost's House.
- Chapel.
- Examination Hall.
- Dining Hall.

Irish country houses: The Great House

Castletown House, Co. Kildare (1722)

- Castletown is the earliest and grandest of Ireland's Palladian country houses.
- Described as 'the finest house Ireland ever saw'.
- It was designed for William Conolly, Speaker of the Irish House of Commons.
- The central block of the house is inspired by Renaissance design.

Castletown House, Co. Kildare

- In true Palladian fashion, the wings contained the kitchens on one side and the stables on the other.
- The wings are connected to the house by curved Ionic colonnades (rows of columns).
- The façade was almost certainly designed by Italian architect Alessandro Galilei.
- Irish architect Sir Edward Lovett Pearce designed the wings, which were later added to the main house.

key point

Visit www.castletownhouse.ie for a tour of the house and a video of every room.

Entrance hall

- Designed by Edward Lovett Pearce.
- Two storeys with Ionic columns and a black-and-white chequered floor.

Stairs

- The staircase is cantilevered (extending outwards, supported only at the wall).
- Made of Portland stone, a pale limestone from Portland, Dorset, south west England.

The Long Gallery

- The decoration was inspired by the excavations at Pompeii at the time.

- A semicircle above the double doors depicts Aurora, Goddess of the Dawn. The image was inspired by a painting by Guido Reni in Rome.
- Three original glass chandeliers from Venice in blue and pink glass still hang.

Russborough House, Co. Wicklow (1741)

- Russborough House is the best-preserved of Ireland's country houses designed by Richard Castle.
- It is in the Palladian style, with the central block and pavilions linked by curved Doric colonnades.

Russborough House, Co. Wicklow

Interior

- All the rooms on the ground floor are cubed to 6 m in length and height.
- Ceilings are coved (curved where wall and ceiling join) to soften the height.
- Mahogany mantelpieces and floors with satinwood inlay feature throughout.
- A collection of paintings belonging to Sir Alfred Beit is on view to the public.

key point

Visit www.russborough.ie for more information.

exam focus

If the colour illustration on your exam paper shows another Georgian country house, make comparisons in your answer with Castletown and Russborough and describe features they would have in common.

Public buildings

Trinity College Dublin

- The college was established by Queen Elizabeth I and Dublin city grew around it.
- A new façade and square were built between 1752 and 1760.
- The new West Front is made of granite with Portland stone columns.
- It has a portico (entrance porch) with six columns in the classical Corinthian style.
- William Chambers designed the Chapel and Public Theatre on either side of the classical Front Square.
- Richard Castle designed the Dining Hall.
- Provost's House (where the president of the college lives) is one of Dublin's grandest Georgian town houses.

Parliament House (Bank of Ireland, College Green)

- Parliament House in Dublin was the first purpose-built parliament house in the world.

- It was designed by Sir Edward Lovett Pearce.
- This was the earliest large-scale Palladian public building in Britain or Ireland.
- Pearce did not live to see his most important work completed. He died in 1733 at the age of thirty-four.

Parliament House (Bank of Ireland, College Green)

- The central section with its splendid piazza and forecourt is surrounded on three sides by Ionic colonnades.

Visit www.archiseek.com for a profile and beautiful pictures of Parliament House.

- It is built of Portland stone.
- James Gandon designed a new portico for the House of Lords in 1785 and linked it to the forecourt with a curved screen wall.
- A similar curved wall was added on the west side in 1803 after the Parliament building was sold to the Bank of Ireland.
- This gave the building its now familiar semicircular appearance.
- The interior of the House of Lords is unchanged from the original.

Town houses in Dublin

After Richard Castle died in 1751, no architect dominated the building style in late eighteenth-century Dublin. Its character was formed instead by rich and influential families.

Examples

- Leinster House (1745–1748): Designed by Richard Castle.
- Charlemont House, now Municipal Gallery of Art (1762–1765): Designed by William Chambers.
- Casino at Marino (late 1750s to c. 1775): Designed by William Chambers.

The Wide Streets Commission (officially the Commissioners for making Wide and Convenient Ways, Streets and Passages) was established by an act of parliament in 1757 at the request of Dublin Corporation. A large part of the old medieval city was demolished to make way for the creation of new wide streets.

Georgian towns

Town planning was particularly concentrated in eighteenth-century England, and Ireland followed suit. Large towns like Dublin saw the development of churches, schools, hospitals and market houses.

Georgian streets and squares

Many Georgian streets still bear the names of the families who developed them. The Fitzwilliam family, Earls of Merrion, developed part of their great estate on the southside of the Liffey in Dublin between 1760 and 1850. The first project was Merrion Street. Fitzwilliam Street, Fitzwilliam Square and Mount Street Upper followed.

key point

Number 29 Fitzwilliam Street is Dublin's Georgian House Museum. Visitors are guided through the house from the basement to the attic, and rooms are furnished as they would have been in the years 1790–1820. Visit the website for a virtual tour of the house:

www.esb.ie/main/about-esb/numbertwentynine/default.htm.

Leinster House

- Originally known as Kildare House.
- James Fitzgerald, the Earl of Kildare, built his town house on the south side of the river, which was unfashionable at that time.
- Designed by Richard Castle.
- The aim was to have the grandest mansion in all of Dublin to reflect Fitzgerald's eminent position in Irish society.
- On Fitzgerald's appointment to Duke of Leinster in 1766, the house was renamed Leinster House.
- Today Leinster House is the site of the Dáil and Seanad.

Charlemont House

- Charlemont House was originally the town house of James Caulfeild, first Earl of Charlemont.
- Caulfield was one of Irelands' great patrons of the arts.
- Charlemont House was designed by William Chambers.
- It became the Municipal Gallery of Modern Art in 1933.

Terraced Houses

- Dublin's Georgian houses are impressive streetscapes of plain red-bricked terraces.
- The Wide Streets Commission had the power to impose uniformity on buildings.
- The house façade, including the spacing and shape of windows, was designed in accordance with classical rules of proportion.
- The principal living space was at first-floor level, so windows are large on this floor.
- The only variation is found in the doorways. Ornate fanlights appear over the doors and patterns can be seen on the first-floor balconies.
- The first floor was sometimes faced in granite.
- Terraced houses were often built in threes by the owner, who later let out the two smaller, plainer houses.

Typical Georgian interior

- The richness of Georgian interiors varied according to the wealth of the owner.
- Typically, the fanlight over the main door lit the hallway and led the entrant straight to the stairs and reception rooms on the first floor.
- The hall was paved in stone, often in black and white squares.
- Doors were often surmounted by elaborate over-doors.
- Drawing-room ceilings usually had the most ornate stucco decoration.

Georgian door, Dublin

Town Houses outside of Dublin

Limerick

The Pery Family has been associated with the city since the seventeenth century. A terrace in Pery Square, Limerick is a fine example of Georgian architecture. Number 2, Pery Square has been fully restored with all its original architectural features expertly reinstated in precise detail. Decor and furnishings are also from the Georgian era.

Pery Square, Limerick

Neoclassical Period: Late eighteenth and early nineteenth centuries

In England, Palladianism was quite suddenly replaced by a purer style based on classical Greek architecture. The change was more gradual in Ireland.

Influences on the style

- Young gentlemen travelled to Italy as part of the 'grand tour' and saw ancient Rome for themselves.
- In England a book called *Antiquities of Athens* was published. It was full of drawings of reconstructions of Greek buildings and it became very popular.

Neoclassical buildings in Dublin

- Blue Coat School: designed by Thomas Ivory (1773).
- The Casino at Marino: designed by William Chambers (1760).
- Custom House: designed by James Gandon (1781).
- Four Courts: designed by James Gandon (1786).
- Portico, Parliament House: designed by James Gandon (1785).

Blue Coat School

- The former Blue Coat School is now occupied by the Law Society of Ireland.
- The building is essentially Palladian, but it has some new details, e.g. blank niches on the main floor and windows.
- This marks the beginning of the Neoclassical style.

James Caulfield (Lord Charlemont)

- James Caulfield, first Earl of Charlemont, was one of Ireland's most enlightened and cultivated men.
- Lord Charlemont was well known for his love of classical art and culture.
- He spent nine years on the Grand Tour of Europe, visiting Rome before travelling on to Greece.
- He collected paintings, books and antique sculptures and had them shipped home.
- He befriended many young architects, painters and *stuccodores*.
- On his return to Ireland, he commissioned William Chambers to design both his town house and country house.
- His country house at Marino was destroyed in a fire, but the Casino in the grounds remains intact.

The Casino at Marino: AD 1760

The Casino at Marino

- The Casino (meaning small house) probably had very little function but it is a perfect gem of architectural design.
- From the outside it appears to be a Greek temple design with one storey, but it has three stories and a basement.
- The second storey is camouflaged behind the large door, of which only half opens.
- Grecian funerary urns function as chimneys throughout.
- The columns are hollow to allow rain to run down and collect in tanks.
- The interior rooms are very small but well-proportioned.
- Ceilings are beautifully ornate with decorative plasterwork.
- Magnificent parquet floors have inlaid patterns in exotic woods.
- The work on the Casino was carried out by Simon Vierpyl, following William Chambers' direction.

Custom House Dublin

Custom House, Dublin

- In 1781 James Gandon was summoned to Dublin to build a new Custom House.
- It was built on slob land that was reclaimed from the estuary of the Liffey when the Wide Streets Commissioners constructed the Quays.
- The large rectangular building has four façades, each one different but linked by corner pavilions.
- The south façade faces the river and its long continuous line is broken by the central bay and portico as well as the two end pavilions.
- The Portico features free-standing Doric columns.
- The exterior is richly adorned with sculpture, most of which is by Edward Smyth.
- The urns on the skyline are similar to those on the Casino at Marino.

Liffey riverine head, Custom House Dublin

- The best-known carvings are the Riverine heads set in the keystones above the doors and windows. They represent the rivers of Ireland and the Liffey, which appears over the main door, is the only female in the series.
- Republican forces burned the Custom House in 1921 and Gandon's original interior was completely destroyed.
- The central dome was rebuilt with native Irish limestone, which is slightly darker than the original Portland stone.

The Four Courts

- The Four Courts were also designed by James Gandon.
- The building was damaged in 1922 when it was burned by Free State troops fighting in the Civil War.
- The original façade has been restored, but the interior was lost.

Portico for the House of Lords

- James Gandon designed the large new portico as a separate entrance for the House of Lords at Parliament House.
- Corinthian-style columns are a feature of the portico.

Stucco (Plasterwork)

Plasterwork is called 'stucco' work after the Italian word *stuccodore*, meaning plasterer. Stucco was very popular in grand Irish houses, in town houses and country houses alike. Some very fine stucco is to be found in Irish Georgian houses and the styles changed over the years from 1725 to 1800.

Stuccodores

Paul and Philip La Francini

- The Francini brothers were brought from Italy to Ireland in 1738 by the Earl of Kildare to execute the great saloon ceiling at Carton House, Co. Kildare.
- They introduced the human figure into plasterwork.
- Most of their work is plain white with high-relief figures, flowers and garlands.
- They worked in the Rococo manner, a style fashionable in most of Europe and associated with swirling ornament.
- The work of the Francini brothers profoundly influenced Irish *stuccodores*.

Robert West

- Robert West was an Irish *stuccodore* who worked in the Rococo manner.
- He produced some of the finest plasterwork in Dublin.

Robert Adam and Michael Stapleton

- Robert Adam was an English architect and furniture designer who developed a style of plasterwork that became popular in England after the 1760s.
- He used moulds to produce low-relief plasterwork in the Neoclassical style.
- Michael Stapleton inherited Robert West's practice and went on to produce sophisticated, delicate work in the Adams style.
- This kind of plasterwork looks very well picked out in colour.
- Examples of this work can be found in many Dublin buildings, including Trinity College and Lucan House (now the Italian Embassy).

Stucco in Irish country houses

Superb examples of La Francini work can be seen at Carton House, Castletown House and Russborough House. Copies of Francini stucco were taken from Riverstown House, Co. Cork in 1948 and they can be seen in a corridor at Áras an Uachtaráin.

Castletown House

- The staircase walls at Castletown House are elaborately decorated with Francini work.
- These feature shells, garlands, Chinese dragons and masks.

Francini stucco on staircase walls at Castletown House

Russborough

- Some of Ireland's finest plasterwork can be found at Russborough House.
- Records of the work were destroyed during the destruction of the Four Courts during the Civil War.
- In the absence of written records, it can only be assumed that stucco on the ceilings of the saloon, library and music room is the work of the Francini brothers.
- The saloon ceiling is filled with garlands of flowers and little putti and the library and stairway are also superbly decorated.

Terraced houses

Magnificent stucco work can be found on the staircases and ceilings of Dublin's terraced houses.

Number 20 Dominick Street

- Robert West built number 20 Dominick Street for himself.
- His extraordinarily rich and imaginative Rococo plasterwork is found on the stairs up to the reception rooms.
- The house is famous for its free-standing, three-dimensional plaster birds.

Belvedere House

- Michael Stapleton's delicately-modelled stucco can be seen at its imaginative best in Belvedere House.
- The walls and ceilings are covered with a rich display of coloured medallions surrounded by lace-like geometric patterns.
- Colour dominates the stairs, ceiling and walls in blue, yellow and pale green as well as russet.

Wedgwood ceiling, Belvedere House

2006 Higher Level paper: Section I, Question 4

Plasterwork (stucco) was a popular decorative feature of the interior of fine Irish Georgian houses of the eighteenth century.

Describe and discuss the decoration, including plasterwork, of the interior of any Georgian country house or town house you have studied

and

Describe at least four common features of the Georgian architectural style.

Illustrate your answer.

The following marking scheme applies to this question:

- Description and discussion of the decoration of a Georgian house: 15 marks.
- Stucco: 10 marks.
- Description of four common features of Georgian architecture: 15 marks.
- Sketches: 10 marks.
- Total: 50 marks.

Tips for answering this question

Use the sample answer at the end of this chapter as a basis for answering this question. However, more attention should be given to one example, such as the interior and plasterwork at Castletown House or at Russborough House.

For part 2 of the question, choose features such as:

- Palladian style: central block building linked to pavilions by curved colonnaded walls, classical columns and pilasters; topped by Ionic, Doric or Corinthian capitols; central porticos with triangular pediments; and rectangular multi-pane windows.
- Terraced red-bricked houses: panelled front doors; fanlight over the door; and black and white chequered floors.

2007 Higher Level paper: Section I, Question 4

The Casino at Marino, designed by William Chambers (1723–1796), is considered to be one of the finest examples of Irish Georgian architecture. Describe and discuss the function, design, exterior architectural features and interior decoration of this building

and

Compare it briefly with one other named Georgian building that you have studied.

Illustrate your answer.

The following marking scheme applies to this question:

- Description and discussion of exterior design and architectural features of the Casino: 15 marks.
- Description and discussion of the interior decoration and function: 10 marks.
- Other named Georgian building: 5 marks.
- Comparison with other building: 10 marks.
- Sketches: 10 marks.
- Total: 50 marks.

2009 Higher Level paper: Section I, Question 5

Russborough House, Co. Wicklow is an example of eighteenth-century architecture.

Name the architect of this building and describe and discuss its style and architectural features

and

Compare it briefly with one other named Georgian building.

Use sketches to illustrate your answer.

The following marking scheme applies to this question:

- Name of architect: 5 marks.
- Description and discussion of illustration referring to style and architectural features: 25 marks.
- Name and brief comparison with other Georgian building: 15 marks.
- Sketches: 5 marks.
- Total: 50 marks.

Most questions on Georgian Ireland focus on architecture. Know enough to be able to answer a question on country houses such as Castletown and Russborough. You should also be familiar with important public buildings like Parliament House, the Custom House, etc. Sometimes questions relate to decoration and plasterwork (2002, 2006) so be prepared for that, too!

SAMPLE EXAM QUESTION

Describe and discuss the use of stucco decoration during the Georgian period, referring in your answer to some important examples, the imagery/motifs used and the visual impact of the stucco decoration on the interiors.

Illustrate your answer.

SAMPLE ANSWER

The Georgian period was a wonderful time for the arts of decoration and architecture in Ireland. An extended period of peace from about 1720 to 1800 resulted in a huge increase in building of houses and public buildings in both in town and country. This was the most elegant and elaborate architecture the country had ever seen.

The design of these new buildings was greatly influenced by sixteenth-century Italian architect Andrea Palladio. He published books that were focused on his work on the classical remains of ancient Rome. A manuscript by the ancient Roman architect Vitruvius was also a guide for the detail and elegance of eighteenth-century designs but because Vitruvius' writings contained no sketches, accounts of his work were broadly interpreted.

Works of remarkable and highly distinctive craftsmanship were being produced in forms such as stonework, silver and glass. These were used to decorate and distinguish Georgian buildings. However, none of these compares in beauty to the elaborate plasterwork that adorns the many wonderful houses of this time.

Stucco Work

This relief wall decoration known as stucco (after the Italian word meaning 'plaster') was very popular in fine houses during the eighteenth century in both England and Ireland. The first style used was the 'compartmented style', which was simply the way in which the ceiling was decorated with geometric shapes. It was the Palladian style, however, that came to dominate the early part of the century.

Francini Brothers

In plasterwork this style used motifs inspired by Greek and Roman decoration. The Francini brothers are very famous *stuccodores* who worked in Ireland during the early eighteenth century. They were brought over from Italy in 1738 and created stucco in many of Ireland's finest country houses. Most of their work was done in plain white in the Rococo manner, a style associated with swirling ornament with high relief figures, flowers and garlands. It was the Francini brothers who introduced the human figure into plasterwork.

The Francini brothers worked in many of the country's grand houses, including Castletown House in Co. Kildare and Russborough House in Co. Wicklow. In Castletown House the walls are elaborately decorated with Chinese dragons, masks, shells and garlands. Classic plasterwork decorates the over doors and the ceiling is divided into ornate compartments. Russborough House has some of Ireland's finest plasterwork. It is done in the Rococo manner and much of it features garlands of flowers and little putti.

Irish Stuccodores

In Ireland, work attributed to the Italians often turns out to be the work of Irishmen who were influenced by them, e.g. Robert West. Robert West is easily the greatest of Irish *stuccodores* and his own home at 20 Lower Dominick Street in Dublin is his flamboyant masterpiece. From the exterior, number 20 looks to be a plain bricked terraced house but the interior presents extraordinarily rich Rococo stucco decoration. On the stairway are his famous three-dimensional birds. With wings outspread, these lifelike creatures are perched 16 inches out from the wall and they give a feeling of elegance and grace. Also included in the decoration are musical instruments and flowers. At each corner of the ceiling pairs of girls appear, whose heads and shoulders emerge from cone-shaped pockets.

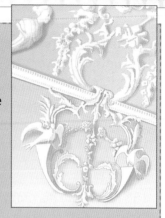

Neoclassicism

Palladianism went out of fashion quite suddenly and from about 1760 to the end of the century the Neoclassical style became popular first in England and then in Ireland. Young men of means took what was known as the 'grand tour', travelling around Europe as part of their education. They sometimes spent years abroad and an important aspect of this was to visit the remains of ancient Rome. By now, travel to Greece had become possible and a newly published book called *Antiquities of Athens* became the inspiration for a new and more authentic classical style of architecture.

Adam Style

The style also influenced plasterwork and moulds were now used to create low-relief, delicate stucco work in what became known as the 'Adam style'. Adam style was named after Englishmen Robert and James Adams and the effect was delicate and more uniform in design, closer to the Classical ideal.

In Ireland, master *stuccodore* Michael Stapleton took over from Robert West and became prominent in the latter half of the eighteenth century. Even though he worked mainly with moulds in the Adams style, some examples of freehand work can also be found.

Coloured Stucco

Neoclassical stucco work is seen at its best when it is picked up in colour. Examples of Michael Stapleton's work can be found in Lucan House, Trinity College Chapel and Belvedere House. Delicately moulded medallions encircled by lace-like patterns are a feature of his work. Belvedere House shows his work at its finest, where coloured plasterwork richly decorates the walls and ceilings and intricate designs and colours dominate. The ceiling is blue, with centrepieces and lacework done in white. The yellow walls have pale green panels and figures done in white, while the frieze is done in a russet colour.

With such mixture of colours and variety of patterns, work like this is a perfect example of the wealth, gaiety, vitality and taste of the Georgian Period at its best. The lacy effect also gave a very grand appearance and this was important at a time when elaborate design and decoration of a house helped to define its owner's social status. In fact, this time of exquisite architecture and plasterwork is often referred to as the 'Irish Renaissance'.

SECTION 2

European Art

Medieval Europe – Chapter 5

The Medieval period is a popular study area. It is a very manageable amount to study and there are very few artist names or art works to be remembered. It focuses mainly on developments in architecture and sculpture as well as the social, cultural, political and religious context in which they took place.

- To gain a clear understanding of the historical background of Medieval Europe
- To fully appreciate the power of the church and its influence on the art and architecture of the period
- To know the technical changes in architecture
- To appreciate the role of art as a narrative medium and a ready source of instruction for the illiterate population
- Be familiar with examples

The Renaissance

The Renaissance is a very long study area. It is almost impossible to cover everything and this seems to have been taken into account on the paper in recent years. There are usually **two questions** on the paper:

- The first (Question 10) tends to relate to the **Early Renaissance in Florence**: painting, sculpture **or** architecture.
- The second (Question 11) tends to relate to the **High Renaissance** but can also relate to the Early Northern Renaissance or later (Germany and England) or Venice.

- To appreciate the concept of the 'Renaissance' as applied to the visual arts
- To understand the influences of classical culture and humanism on painting, sculpture and architecture
- To have gained an understanding of the role of patronage in the City States and the Papacy
- To know and understand the importance artistic status of Italy
- To appreciate the new status in the representation of the human figure in art
- To understand the changed role of the artist

Impressionism and Twentieth-Century Art Movements

The developments in painting in late 19th Century France is a very interesting study area and offers an excellent opportunity to look and respond to paintings of pleasant everyday scenes.

It is however important to fully understand what the concepts that the artists had in mind and what they were trying to achieve.

It is also an area where descriptive language is important because the paintings are quite hard to sketch.

- To understand the beginnings of a modern approach to art
- To explore the effect that historical and political events had on art
- To examine how traditions in art were overturned
- To understand the position of art in society
- To become familiar with the Impressionist style, artists and key paintings
- To have an awareness of 20th century art movements and how they developed

Romanesque art and architecture: Eleventh and twelfth centuries

Romanesque art dominated virtually all of Western Europe from around A.D. 1000 until around A.D. 1200. Romanesque art originated in France but it made a strong impact in Italy and Germany also. The term 'Romanesque' literally means 'Roman-like' and it was first used in the eighteenth century by a French art expert. The term has been used to describe this style ever after.

Life in Medieval Europe

Life in Medieval Europe saw some interesting social changes, including:

- Growth in the economy.
- Renewed energy in learning, philosophy and technology.
- A huge building boom, particularly in churches.
- Stronger social influence from the church and monastic orders.
- Deep engagement with spiritual matters: pilgrimages, devotion to the saints, a reverence towards religious relics, etc.

> **key point**
>
> There was a deep belief in the afterlife throughout all levels of society in Medieval Europe. In a time of great piety, religious observance controlled every aspect of daily life from the cradle to the grave.

Building of churches

There was a dramatic increase in the number of churches built at this time.

- Cluny Abbey in France was rebuilt in the new Romanesque style.

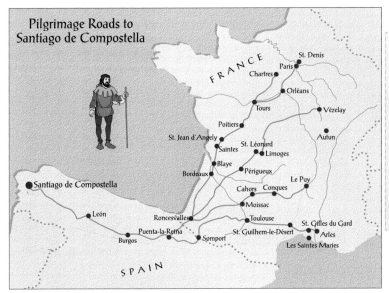

Pilgrimage Roads to Santiago de Compostella

Pilgrimage routes throughout France

> **key point**
>
> The new millennium had an effect on Medieval European society. There was a widespread fear that the world would end in the year A.D. 1000 and this led to a great deal of pessimism about the future during the late 900s.

- Pilgrimages became very popular, e.g. Santiago de Compostela in Spain. As a result, many new churches were built along the four main pilgrimage routes.
- Churches along the pilgrimage routes were built in stone and were very similar in design.

Architecture

- Blocky in shape, giving a solid geometrical appearance.
- Cruciform-shaped ground plan based on the Roman basilica shape with added crosswise transepts.
- Rounded arches (based on Roman arches).
- Stone roofs needed to combat the problem of fire.
- Barrel vaulting, which developed into groin vaulting in later times.
- Outward thrust caused by pressure from the heavy stone roof.
- Very thick walls to support heavy vaults.
- Solid rounded pillars to support stone roofs.
- Dark interiors caused by the high, small windows.
- Ambulatory for pilgrims to walk around.
- A ring of smaller chapels called radiating chapels (*rayonnant* in French) extending out from the ambulatory.
- Large western façades with semi-circular tympanum over the door.

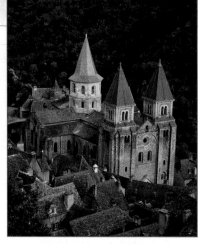

St Foy of Conques, a typical Romanesque church

key point

Barrel and groin vaults were supported in the middle by transverse arches, but the heavy stones pushed down on the arches, causing them to flatten and the walls to buckle outward. This pressure outward is known as outward thrust.

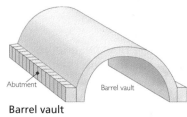

Abutment   Barrel vault

Barrel vault

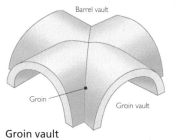

Barrel vault

Groin   Groin vault

Groin vault

Romanesque arch

keystone
voussoir
impost
pier
foundation

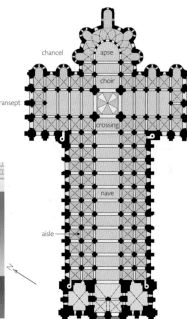

chancel   apse
choir
transept
crossing
nave
aisle

Plan of St Sernin, Toulouse

Sculpture

- Architectural sculpture served the purpose of educating the people.
- Relief sculpture features in the tympanum.
- The Last Judgment is a common theme.
- Grotesque imagery is a feature throughout.
- Carved capitals appear on supporting pillars.
- Sculpture was painted at the time.
- The art is quite abstract and very little realism was attempted.
- Foliage (plants) and drapery (clothing) were treated in a very decorative manner with swirling patterns.
- Figures are sometimes blocky but often elongated.

Exam questions are unlikely to focus on Romanesque architecture alone. It is more common to be asked about the relationship between Romanesque architecture and sculpture, or for a comparison of Romanesque and Gothic styles.

It is not enough to be familiar with just one example of Romanesque sculpture. The exam question may ask you to discuss several examples, so study each of the following: tympanum and capitals in Autun; tympanum and capitals in Vézelay; and tympanum in St Foy.

Useful resources

- Visit www.sacred-destinations.com, following the links for Cluny, Autun, Vézelay and Conques. You will find excellent illustrations and descriptions of important sites of church architecture and sculpture.
- Visit www.wga.hu. Use the search facility to find Gislebertus and you'll see wonderfully detailed images of the tympanum at Autun. You should also search for Vézelay.

St Foy de Conques

St Foy de Conques is a typical Romanesque pilgrimage church. It was a popular stopping point for pilgrims on the way to Santiago de Compostela. The church houses the relic of St Foy, a young woman martyred for her faith.

Architecture

- Blocky and geometric in appearance.
- Rounded arches on windows, doorways and supporting piers.
- Thick walls support a high stone barrel-vaulted roof.
- Small windows make the interior quite dark.
- A very large dome over the crossing brings in good light.
- The main western façade is large, simple and geometric in design.

Sculpture

- A tympanum over the main door has a relief sculpture of the Last Judgment.
- This is a particularly expressive scene, with Christ in the centre raising his hand in blessing.
- To the right of Christ is a detailed depiction of heaven, with realistic figures of the apostles and a procession of saints.
- To the left of Christ is a graphic depiction of the torment of sinners condemned to hell.
- The upper level shows the weighing of souls and beyond the gates below are devils pushing the damned into snarling jaws.
- An inscription in Latin translates as: 'O sinners, if you do not mend your ways, know that you will suffer a dreadful fate.'
- The sculpture was originally painted and some colour is still visible on sheltered spots.

> **key point**
>
> Medieval architectural sculptures like the Last Judgment at St Foy are sometimes referred to as 'sermons in stone'.

St Magdalene, Vézelay

This is the largest Romanesque church in France. It was a Benedictine abbey overseen by Cluny and it housed a relic of Mary Magdalene. It was officially listed by Cluny as a major stopping point on the route to Santiago de Compostela.

Architecture

- Exterior damaged during the French Revolution.
- Interior very well preserved.
- Rebuilt around A.D. 1150, after a fire killed twelve hundred pilgrims.

Interior

- Groin-vaulting.
- Rounded arches divide the nave.
- Ochre and white stone on the arches give a unique chequered effect.
- Arches supported with square piers with engaged (attached) rounded pillars on each side.
- Noticeable sagging outwards of the walls (outward thrust).
- Buttresses later added to the exterior to prevent further outward thrust.

Sculpture

Tympanum

- Carved relief sculpture on the tympanum inside the narthex (porch).
- The tympanum sculpture depicts the Pentecost or descent of the Holy Spirit upon the apostles fifty days after the resurrection of Christ.
- The large figure of Christ is enclosed in a mandorla (oval halo) with arms open.

- The light of the Holy Spirit falls from Christ's hands onto the heads of the apostles.
- Above and below Christ is a representation of all of humanity.

Carved capitals in the Nave

- Capitals in the nave are carved on three sides and the imagery is typically Romanesque in its fascination with the grotesque.
- *The Mystic Mill* is Vézelay's most famous capital. It shows Moses pouring grain (which symbolises the law) into a mill (symbolising Christ), while St Paul the Apostle gathers the flour.

Tympanum at St Magdalene at Vézelay

St Lazare, Autun

St Lazare is one of the most important Romanesque churches in France. It was built in the mid-twelfth century. Some later Gothic additions were needed–the great spire was added after a fire in the fifteenth century–but the core of the church remains Romanesque. It is famous for its wonderful sculptures by Gislebertus.

Sculpture

Tympanum

- Carved relief sculpture on the west tympanum.
- The tympanum sculpture depicts the Last Judgment.
- In the centre, Christ sits impassively inside a great mandorla held by angels.
- An inscription in Latin below Christ's feet identifies the sculptor with the words 'Gislebertus hoc fecit' or 'Gislebertus made this'.
- To Christ's right, the apostles incline their heads towards him.

The Mystic Mill,
capital at Vézelay

key point

The simplicity of the storytelling sculpture at Autun tends to appeal to the modern viewer not just because of its intensity but because its expressive, elongated figures have a distinctly abstract quality.

- St Peter holds a large key and turns to welcome the souls of the saved into heaven.
- On the lintel below, all the souls arise from their coffins.
- An angel with a flaming sword separates the saved from the damned.
- The saved on Christ's right rejoice and look towards him, while the souls of the damned stumble off naked.
- Amongst the saved, an angel guides three children upwards.
- Two pilgrims walk upwards towards Christ. They carry bags showing symbols: the cross for the pilgrimage to Jerusalem and a scallop shell representing Santiago de Compostela.

- Among the damned is a miser with heavy money bags and an adulteress with snakes gnawing at her.
- A pair of giant hands grips a tormented soul to pull it upwards.
- The weighing of souls is depicted. Archangel Michael leans on the scales to help them go in the right direction.
- A devil sits in the scales and another pulls on it to make it heavier.
- Souls are poured down the chute into the jaws of hell, while a devil leans out to torment them.

Tympanum at Autun

key point

The tympanum at Autun was plastered over in the mid-eighteenth century because the church had grown embarrassed by its harsh imagery. The head of Christ was sticking out so it was hacked off. The plaster was removed in 1837 and Christ's head was found in a local museum in 1948. Because the tympanum was plastered over it survived the Revolution, while many other artworks were lost.

Pilgrims detail, tympanum at Autun

Carved Capitals

- The capitals show Gislebertus' skills as a sculptor and storyteller.
- Some of the best examples can be seen on the pillars of the choir, which was replaced after a fire and is now in the museum of the cathedral.
- *The Suicide of Judas* is a famous carved capital. It depicts Judas hanging himself after betraying Jesus. Hideous devils pull on Judas's rope. The horror of the event contrasts with a beautifully depicted ornamental tree and the scene fits neatly into the shape of the capital.

The Dream of the Magi, Autun

- *The Dream of the Magi* is another fascinating capital. Few details convey the message of the scene very clearly. Here we see the angel pointing to the star of Bethlehem. The three kings sleep in one cosy bed, wearing their crowns. The angel gently touches the hand of one sleeping king, warning him not to return to Herod but to follow the star. The king wakes from his sleep, one eye open.

SAMPLE EXAM QUESTION

Describe and discuss in detail the work of Gislebertus. Refer to the stylistic, narrative and expressive qualities of the work.

SAMPLE ANSWER

We may have never known it was Gislebertus who sculpted some of the most beautiful work in the twelfth century if it were not for the tympanum in the Cathedral of St Lazare in Autun in France. In an extremely rare occurrence in medieval art, the inscription 'Gislebertus Hoc Fecit' ('Gislebertus made this') appears on the sculpture beneath the feet of Christ, suggesting that this is the signature of the artist.

During the Romanesque period, the church was the most powerful institution and Church leaders encouraged people to make pilgrimages to Santiago de Compostela in northern Spain. Building was booming as roads, bridges and particularly churches were built to serve the needs of the thousands of pilgrims on the move throughout Europe.

Romanesque

The word 'Romanesque' means 'Roman-like' and these churches were designed like older Roman basilicas. Church building reached great heights in France where five new churches were built on each of four main pilgrimage routes. One of these was at Autun in the Burgundy region.

Autun

A large carved scene on the great semicircular tympanum over the main doorway at Autun depicts the Last Judgment. Such a scene would not have been unusual, but the grotesque imagery here is particularly dramatic and realistic. It was most probably sculpted to scare pilgrims to change their ways lest they be destined for hell.

Part of this scene includes the Weighing of Souls, which is probably the most famous of all Romanesque sculptures. A huge figure of a judgmental God sits on a throne in the centre, while underneath the souls rise from their tombs as angels sound the last trumpet. To the right of God, Peter welcomes the saved souls to heaven; to the left of God, hideous devils wrestle for the souls of those who are being weighed before the damned are dragged off to hell by grotesque demons.

Gislebertus

Gislebertus has an abstract, figurative style. We can see this by his elongated, non-naturalistic figures on the tympanum. The impassive Archangel Michael weighs the souls while terrified figures hide beneath his robes. An evil-looking devil with long hairy legs and hooves tries to pull down the scale, while another sits in it to make it heavier before a laughing demon pours those condemned forever down a chute towards the gaping jaws of hell and the fires below.

Although this part of the tympanum is quite grotesque overall, Gislebertus also tries to inspire hope and comfort to pilgrims. Along the lintel below the feet of Christ, giant hands grip a tormented soul and various forms of sin are depicted. We see the miser with his heavy money bags and the adulteress being gnawed by snakes. However, there are also pilgrims on their way to heaven gazing upwards. The cross symbolising Jerusalem and the shell symbolising St James of Santiago de Compostela appear on the pilgrims' satchels and help us identify them. Here also is an angel guiding three children towards heaven. This  image must have greatly comforted those whose children had died.

This being said, Gislebertus does not hold back in making the devils and hell scene as horrible as possible. We see that he is very creative and imaginative in his work.

The Capitals

The capitals on the supporting piers inside the cathedral were all carved by Gislebertus himself and show fine ornamental foliage and expertly fashioned figures. However, their key element is the story itself and the simplicity of its telling. The main purpose of Medieval art was didactic. Everything that people needed to know about their religion was contained in the sculpture in the churches. It focused mainly on the stories from the Bible and from his work we can see that Gislebertus was a fine storyteller.

'The Suicide of Judas' is certainly one of the most gruesome images at Autun. Judas hangs grotesquely from a beautifully depicted tree, helped by two hideous devils who seem to gloat and laugh. The detailed expressive qualities on the faces of these figures add to the drama of the scene, but all three as well as the tree are skillfully composed to fit the shape of the capitol.

Although the facial expressions of his figures are detailed, Gislebertus keeps his narrative capitals clear and direct and ensures that fancy complications are kept to a minimum. Complicated figures might have got in the way of the story, which was the main purpose of the sculpture.

Gislebertus also shows a gentle side. On another of Autun's capitals, an image of the Three Kings asleep is charming in its simplicity. Once again this group of figures is very cleverly designed to fit the awkward shape. Sharing the one cosy bed and still wearing their crowns, the kings sleep beneath a magnificent semicircular bedcover. One king opens an eye in response to the touch of the angel who is pointing upwards towards the star. It is a reminder of the one that led the kings to Bethlehem, but the angel is now warning them not to return to Herod. This same simplicity is also seen in the capital of the Holy Family on their way to Egypt on the donkey. Joseph leads the little group and although Mary's pose is very stiff and the child quite solemn, the donkey is very naturally portrayed and may even be smiling a little.

Gislebertus's work can still be seen today. It is amazing how it has lasted from the twelfth century. This is because the Church plastered over the tympanum before the French Revolution, as it was ashamed of the crude, vulgar imagery. The plaster was removed in the nineteenth century, revealing the sculpture in almost perfect condition.

Sinéad Crowley, 2010

key point

Some of the material on Gislebertus's work could be included in other essays relating to Romanesque sculpture. Instead of writing only about Autun, compare the scene on the tympanum at Autun with that of Vézelay or St Foy. Make comparisons also between the sculptured capitals of both of these churches.

Question

Romanesque sculpture had decorative and narrative functions.

Discuss this statement in relation to two named examples of Romanesque sculpture you have studied. Emphasise the treatment of the human figure in your answer

and

Name a Romanesque church you have studied and discuss briefly the relationship between its architecture and sculpture.

Illustrate your answer.

SAMPLE ANSWER

- *Your answer for the **first part of the question** could include a comparison with sculpture in Vézelay.*

Sample paragraph

From research, I found out that Gislebertus trained at Cluny and probably worked as an assistant at Vézelay in the Cathedral of St Magdalen. However, I think that

Gislebertus could have been more than an assistant at Vézelay because I find the two tympanums extremely similar.

Both have powerful Christ figures sitting in the centre, arms outstretched. Both are surrounded by elongated abstract figures. Although, perhaps this was just the style of the time, because surely Gislebertus would have signed his work at Vézelay?

TIP

- Here a description and sketch of the tympanum at Vézelay should be included, before moving on to a comparison with *The Mystic Mill* capital.

On the other hand, *The Mystic Mill* capital in Vézelay is quite different to those found in Autun, such as The Three Kings. The figures in the Vézelay capital are more detailed and also more realistic.

TIP

- Here a description and sketch of *The Mystic Mill* capital should be provided.
- Your answer for the **second part of the question** could begin with an introduction similar to this:

Introduction

During a period of peace after much turmoil in Medieval Europe the population began to grow, new trade and ideas began to flourish and the Christian Church rose to a position of great power.

The Church promoted pilgrimages to the ordinary people as a means of penance for their sins and work towards gaining a place in heaven in the afterlife. Building was taking place at an enormous rate and nowhere was this more obvious than in the building of new churches to accommodate the huge numbers of travelling pilgrims and growing congregations.

Romanesque was the name given in the nineteenth century to the dominant style of art and architecture during the eleventh and twelfth centuries. This is because of the many similarities between this style and the Roman style. Medieval churches used the same ground plan as the Roman basilica but added transepts to give it the shape of a cross. Rounded Roman arches were widely used on doors and windows.

Romanesque churches were also the first since Roman times to use sculpture as decoration. Roman works of art, particularly free-standing figures of gods and goddesses, were viewed with great suspicion by the Church and considered pagan, even dangerous. Christian sculptors therefore opted to cover the façades of churches with relief sculpture instead. Similarities can be found between some Romanesque churches and the sculpture on Roman triumphal arches. This is especially notable of churches in the south of France. However, instead of depicting glorious deeds of battle, sculpture on Romanesque churches depicted stories from the Bible.

Sculpture to educate

At the time, very few people could read or write, so the church used this sculpture to educate them in the important points of their religion. Life expectancy was low and fear of death was constant, so the main theme of the sculpture was often a reminder for people to repent of their sins in preparation for the next life.

The most popular Christian pilgrimage was to Santiago de Compostela, where the body of St James the apostle had recently been discovered. Churches were built all along four main pilgrimage routes in France and many of these became special places of pilgrimage in their own right. All churches had relics of the saints and the more important the relic, the more pilgrims came to pray.

St Magdalene of Vézelay and St Lazare of Autun are striking examples of Romanesque churches. Both were very important destinations on the pilgrimage routes and both possess exceptionally fine sculpture.

Caitriona Ahern, 2010

- Following this introduction, you could provide detailed descriptions and sketches of two sculptures from St Magdalene of Vézelay and/or St Lazare of Autun.
- To discuss the relationship between architecture and sculpture, you could include the following points:
  - None of the carving is free-standing, so it could be described as decoration on the architecture.
  - Although the figures are carved in high relief, they are designed to fit the shape of the tympanum.
  - The pillars that form part of the structure have decorated capitals. These are also designed to fit a shape dictated by the structure of the architecture.
  - The quality of the sculpture and its narrative function distinguishes it from merely decorative art to some of the finest art in western culture.
- A possible example for discussion: Describe the sculpture at St Magdalene of Vézelay as part of the overall architectural decoration that includes pink and white coloured stone on the arches.

Gothic art and architecture: Thirteenth and fourteenth centuries

The beginnings of Gothic

The Gothic style began in France in the middle of the twelfth century. Abbot Suger began the restoration of the Benedictine Abbey of St Denis in Paris and combined features of Romanesque architecture, like the cross-ribbed vault and the pointed arch, in a new way.

His innovations had far-reaching developments in architecture, sculpture and stained glass and his ideas soon spread to the area around Paris known as the *Île de France*. St Denis was badly damaged during the French Revolution, so the best example of a Gothic cathedral is Chartres. The Gothic style later became popular all over Europe.

> **key point**
>
> None of the features of Gothic architecture were new; all had been used already in Romanesque. However, the unique combination of these features in the Gothic style made for a completely new way of building.

The Gothic cathedral

During the thirteenth century important towns in France like Chartres, Tours, Orléans, Amiens and Reims each had its own great cathedral. Cathedrals served two important purposes in a town:

- They were the most important status symbol of the town.
- They helped to educate people in their religion though Bible stories featured in the sculpture and glass.

Gothic architecture

Gothic architecture possesses distinctive features:

- Pointed arch.
- Ribbed vault.
- Flying buttress.
- Ambulatory with radiating chapels.

Pointed arches

Ribbed vault

transverse ridge rib

longitudinal ridge rib

Panel

Rib vault

Gothic Tracery

Rose window

Flying butress

- Clustered columns supporting ribs spreading in different directions.
- Large *clerestory* (upper level) windows, which could be inserted because of flying buttresses.
- Large, round 'rose' windows.
- Tracery and window moulding.

Contrast with Romanesque

- **Pointed arches** were stronger than the rounded Romanesque arch.
- **Rib vaulting** (crosswise vaulting) was a more effective system of supporting stone roofs.
- **Buttresses** and **flying buttresses** supported the walls and solved the problem of outward thrust.
- **Slender pillars** could now support the vaulting system.
- **Thinner walls** allowed for building of much greater height and elegance than Romanesque.
- **Windows could be bigger and could allow** more light than in Romanesque buildings.
- **Windows were filled with coloured stained glass.**
- **Tracery** was ornamental stonework used to support the glass in the windows. It gave them a light and delicate appearance.

Be aware of the different styles within Gothic!

Question 8 on the 2008 Higher Level paper expected you to know the names of each cathedral illustrated on the accompanying coloured sheet and to identify the style of Gothic displayed.

As Gothic architecture developed, a sequence of styles evolved:

- Early Gothic, twelfth century: West façade of Chartres Cathedral.
- High Gothic, thirteenth century: Chartres Cathedral; Notre Dame Cathedral, Paris.
- Rayonnant Gothic, late thirteenth century: Reims Cathedral; Sainte Chapelle, Paris.
- Late or Flamboyant Gothic, fourteenth century: Rouen Cathedral.

The word rayonnant in French means deviating and it can describe a development in style. It has nothing at all to do with radiating or 'Rayonnant' chapels found around the choir in most Romanesque and early Gothic churches!

Chartres Cathedral

Chartres Cathedral or *Notre Dame de Chartres* is the best preserved of the major French cathedrals, with its sculpture and most of its original stained glass still intact.

key point

Chartres Cathedral is unique in that it was not destroyed or damaged during the French Revolution. While there have been many restorations over the years, these have not altered its great beauty. It remains today one of the finest examples of thirteenth-century High Gothic architecture, sculpture and glass.

Chartres Cathedral–West facade

The Relic of the Virgin Mary: Sancta Camisia

- The cathedral is dedicated to the Virgin Mary and it was a major pilgrimage site.
- Its most sacred relic was the *Sancta Camisia*, said to be the gown worn by the Virgin Mary during childbirth.

A New Cathedral

- The old Romanesque cathedral was destroyed by fire in 1194 and it was thought the relic was lost. The relic was found three days later and it was taken as a sign to build a new and better cathedral.

Structure

- Most of the original twelfth-century west façade survived the fire; the remainder of the cathedral dates from the thirteenth century.
- The south spire is the original plain, early-Gothic pyramid dating from the 1140s.
- Following a lightning strike in 1506, the north tower was replaced with a taller spire in Flamboyant Gothic style.

Flying buttresses

- Chartres was one of the first large buildings to make full use of flying buttresses.

Interior

- The interior has a central aisle and transepts forming the shape of a cross.
- Slender columns soar dramatically upwards to support the rib vaulting.
- The large upper windows, three great rose windows (round) over the west door and both transepts further intensify the feeling of light and space.

Chartres interior–rib vaulting

The Royal Portal

- The main doorway is called the 'Royal Portal' because of its sculpture.
- Three entrance doors are framed on both sides by rows of tall figures of kings and queens.
- These column statues are some of the most famous sculptures in western art.

Notre Dame Cathedral, Paris

- Notre Dame Cathedral was rebuilt in the thirteenth century, when Paris was developing as the main centre of political power and commerce.
- Part of the Cathedral is early Gothic but numerous architects worked on the site. This resulted in several different styles being incorporated before the cathedral was finally completed around 1345.

Reims Cathedral

Reims Cathedral

- Built in 1210 after a fire destroyed the original, Reims Cathedral is a later, more developed Gothic style known as 'Rayonnant style'.
- Some of its finest Gothic architectural features include: flying buttresses; very thin walls; and complicated, delicate tracery on the windows.
- The cathedral was badly damaged during World War I, but much of its sculpture survived.
- The façade has been very well restored.
- Statues on the sides of the doorways are original.
- It was intended that there be seven towers but only two on the western facade were completed and the spires were never built.

Dedicated to the Virgin Mary

- Instead of the traditional tympanum, the main doorway at Reims is surmounted by a rose window framed by a triangular sculptured arch.
- Mary is the central figure in this sculpture.

Coronations of Kings

- Reims is famous for its association with royalty and all the kings of France from the ninth to the nineteenth century were crowned here.

Sainte Chapelle, Paris

- The little chapel of Sainte Chapelle in Paris is a tiny but perfect example of the Rayonnant style of French Gothic architecture.

Rouen Cathedral

Rouen Cathedral is an example of late or Flamboyant Gothic style.

Rouen Cathedral

Flamboyant is the name given to a decorative style of late Gothic architecture of the fifteenth century. This can be seen in the highly ornamental tracery on the windows and stonework on the façade that has an almost lacelike appearance.

Gothic sculpture

A change came about during the twelfth century in ordinary people's attitude to God. This was because of a softer attitude in church teaching.

Rouen Cathedral is featured in some very famous images by French Impressionist artist Claude Monet. He painted the cathedral in different lights at different times of the day.

Transition from Romanesque

- A more hopeful message is clearly seen in the art of the new Gothic cathedrals.
- This contrasts with the grotesque and frightening imagery of the Romanesque.
- Judgment scenes have not disappeared but they tend to be far less obvious.
- Devotion to the Virgin Mary became very popular.
- This was the era of chivalry and the knightly code of behaviour involved great respect for women.
- Mary's honour was highest of all and she occupies a very prominent position in the sculpture.
- The emphasis is also on Christ as the saviour of mankind.

Make sure you can discuss the development of Gothic sculpture and be familiar with examples of early and later style. Compare and contrast in your answer!

The Saint

- Medieval people loved their saints.
- They prayed to particular saints in times of sickness or distress, appealing to them intercede with God.
- People knew the stories of saints' lives and miracles.
- Numerous images of saints are found in Gothic sculpture and stained glass.
- Ordinary people were familiar with the lives of saints so they found these easy to 'read'.
- Saints in art were identified by their symbols or instruments of their deaths.
- Thirteenth-century sculptors also began to show facial expressions in their sculptures.

Column Statues

- Column statues of kings and queens were common in early Gothic imagery.
- Column statues around the door at St Denis that may have been associated with the French Royal family were destroyed during the Revolution.
- The *Royal Portal* at Chartres Cathedral is very famous for its column statues.
- As Gothic sculpture developed, the figures became more free-standing and naturalistic with more realistic poses.
- Gothic sculpture came to rely less on the supporting architecture.
- Expressions on the faces of statues became more natural; some appear to be smiling.

Sculpture at Chartres

The Royal Portal: Early Gothic, Twelfth Century

- The theme of the *Royal Portal* is salvation. In the central tympanum, Christ in Majesty welcomes the visitor.
- The scenes over the side doors are that of the Virgin Mary and the Ascension of Christ.
- Nobody is quite sure who the column statues of kings and queens on either side of the doorways represent.
- The kings and queens may be kings and queens of Judea or Christ's royal ancestors from the Old Testament.

Royal Portal, Chartres

- These sculptures show development from the Romanesque.
- They are an important part of the overall design of the doorway, blending with and adding to the architecture.
- The folds in the drapery tend to emphasise their tall, linear quality.
- Their facial expressions are serene and dignified.
- Special care has been taken with details such as braided hair; long, flowing sleeves; and girdles.

The Master Sculptor

- Differences in quality can easily be seen between the figures of the three doors.
- The master sculptor is credited with carving the central doorway.
- Assistants may have worked on the doors to the right and left.

The North Portal: High Gothic, Thirteenth Century

- The North Portal is dedicated to the Virgin Mary and in the central tympanum above she is crowned Queen of Heaven.

- Mary is the link and on both sides of the doorways are the prophets who foretold the coming of Christ, alongside the apostles.

Old Testament and New Testament Figures

- Abraham from the Old Testament features. He was willing to sacrifice his beloved son Isaac.
- Opposite is John the Baptist, who foretells the sacrifice of Christ.

Individual Personalities

- These figures are treated very much as individuals and have natural facial expressions and gestures.
- This the first time this was seen in French sculpture.

St Modeste

- The graceful image of St Modeste stands at the corner.
- It is considered one of the most beautiful statues in the cathedral.
- St Modeste is a local saint who was martyred for her faith.
- She holds a book in one hand and raises the other in blessing as she turns her head in a gesture of gentle refinement.

The South Portal: High Gothic, Thirteenth Century

- The south portal is dedicated to Jesus Christ. His church and apostles are on either side of him in the central doorway.

The Teacher

- Jesus stands on the central trumeau with a book in one hand and the other hand lifted in blessing.
- He is represented as a teacher with a gentle facial expression.
- Behind his head is his symbol: the cruciform halo.

Christ's Apostles

- The apostles stand on beautiful twisted columns.
- Each apostle has an identifying symbol.
- St Peter has curly hair and a beard. He carries a key as the symbol of his power on earth.
- St Andrew has a cross.
- St John appears as a beardless youth carrying a book.

Jesus Christ, central trumeau, south portal Chartres Cathedral

key point

The south portal has a Last Judgment scene. It shows the familiar imagery of Michael weighing the souls as devils fight for them. It is a far less graphic representation than those found on earlier Romanesque churches.

Sculpture at Reims Cathedral

- Reims Cathedral is dedicated to the Virgin Mary.
- Her image as Queen of Heaven is seen in the gable above the doorway.
- She appears again on the central pier of the main doorway, welcoming the faithful.
- The Visitation and Annunciation are represented among the statues around the door.
- These figures of Mary and Elizabeth are clearly inspired by Roman sculpture.

> **key point**
>
> Angel Gabriel from the Annunciation is the famous smiling Angel of Reims. This is the emblem for the city.

Gothic Sculpture in Germany

- As the Gothic style spread from France, many new and magnificent cathedrals were built in the French style during the thirteenth century in neighbouring countries like England, Spain and the German Rhineland.
- Artists travelled to other countries, bringing their skills to local artists.
- One of these was a talented sculptor known only as the Naumburg Master. He is thought to have trained in France, but his most famous work is in St Peter and Paul's Cathedral at Naumburg.

Ekehard and Uta

Ekehard and Uta

- The Naumburg Master produced twelve exceptionally fine figures representing the founders of the cathedral.
- The most famous of these are Count Ekehard and his wife Uta.
- The clothing, faces and hands are all carved with very fine detail.
- The poses and gestures have a particularly convincing, real human quality.
- Both figures still retain a good deal of their original bright colouring.

> **key point**
>
> The figure of Uta with her veil and golden crown is said to have influenced Walt Disney in the creation of queens for his films.

Late Gothic Sculpture: Fourteenth Century

By the fourteenth century much had changed. Towns had developed and people lived more independently of the church and the feudal Lords. Art was now produced for the private homes and chapels of wealthy people living in the town.

Curved statuettes

- Small statuettes in curved poses were very popular.
- Figures were also much more human, e.g. sculpture in ivory of the Virgin and Child from the Sainte Chapelle, Paris.

The Virgin of Notre Dame, Paris

- This large statue was made for a small church in the centre of Paris in the middle of the fourteenth century. It was transferred to Notre Dame in the nineteenth century to replace one destroyed during the Revolution.
- The figure is curved and both mother and baby are quite naturalistic.

Claus Sluter, Burgundy

- Claus Sluter came from Haarlem in Holland to work in France for the Dukes of Burgundy.
- His most famous work was made for the Carthusian Monastery located just outside Dijon.

The Well of Moses: Late fourteenth century

- The *Well of Moses* fountain was damaged during the French Revolution but still shows the excellence of Sluter's work.
- The crucifixion scene that was on top of the fountain was destroyed, but the lower half with six life-size figures and weeping angels remains.
- Traces of the original paint can still be seen on the carved stone.
- The figures are the prophets from the Old Testament.
- All are extremely lifelike and realistically portrayed.
- Faces and details of the clothes, such as belts, are particularly real.
- Moses with a wrinkled brow and long beard is dressed in a long, flowing garment.

Well of Moses fountain, Claus Sluter

Gothic stained glass

Stained glass had been used in the Romanesque period, but the technique developed during the Gothic era and was far more widely used.

- It is not known exactly where the technique came from, but the Abbot Suger at St Denis was the first to explore its possibilities.
- Abbot Suger employed skilled craftsmen from abroad.
- He believed that the beauty of stained glass would lift men's souls closer to God.
- He used the glass as a means to tell stories and to help with the instruction of the illiterate population.

exam focus

Make sure you have enough information to answer a full question on stained glass only, e.g. Question 8 on the 2006 Higher Level paper. Select specific examples to study: choose a rose window and compare it to the *Blue Virgin* of Chartres; or compare the glass of Chartres Cathedral to that in Sainte Chapelle, Paris.

Stained glass at Chartres Cathedral

- The windows of Chartres Cathedral are some of the oldest and most beautiful in Europe.
- It is one of the most complete collections of medieval stained glass in the world.
- Portraits on the lower window panel identify individuals or groups who paid for each window of the cathedral.

key point

Chartres retains 152 of its original 186 windows. This is the greatest collection of medieval stained glass in France and is the source of much of our knowledge about its manufacture.

Stories in the glass

- The tall, pointed, long windows around the nave are called *lancet* windows.
- The very large windows at the upper level of the nave are called *clerestory* windows.
- Each window tells a story. Some are relatively easy to 'read' like those of popular, well-known saints. Some are not so clear today because they reflect older church teachings.

Rose windows

- There are three large 'rose windows' at Chartres.
- They are called this because of their shape.
- One is found on each of the side transepts and over the west door on the main façade.
- The transept windows tell stories of Jesus Christ and of the Virgin Mary.
- The western rose depicts scenes from the Last Judgment.

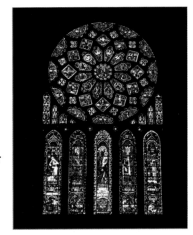

Rose window, Chartres Cathedral

The Blue Virgin window

- The most famous window at Chartres is known as the *Blue Virgin*.
- This lancet window is found behind the altar.
- Mary is portrayed as a queen and her lap forms a throne for her child.
- She is depicted as Queen of Heaven with angels all around and Queen of Earth with authority over demons.
- The central part of the window dates from the twelfth century and it survived the fire in 1194.

Blue Virgin window, Chartres Cathedral

Fourteenth-century stained glass: Sainte Chapelle, Paris

Interior Upper Chapel, Sainte Chapelle

- King Louis IX had Sainte Chapelle built as his own private chapel and he used it to house his most precious relic–a fragment of the crown of thorns worn by Jesus.
- The King paid a large sum of money to buy these relics in 1239 and he wanted Sainte Chapelle to be perfect.
- The interior is full of light and colour from the exquisite stained glass that completely surrounds the walls on three sides.
- The tall, thin lancet windows are coloured in deep reds and blues that blend together to give a purplish hue.
- A rose window was added in the fifteenth century.
- Structural supports have been kept to the bare minimum to accommodate this huge expanse of stained glass.
- The overall effect is one of fragile beauty.
- Sainte Chapelle suffered major damage during the Revolution, but the windows survived.
- Most of Louis IX's collection of precious relics was scattered, but a few remaining fragments can be seen in the treasury of Notre Dame Cathedral.
- Restoration on the chapel took place in the nineteenth century.

2006 Ordinary Level paper: Section II, Question 8

Choose either a Romanesque church or Gothic cathedral that you have studied and answer (a), (b) **and** (c).

(a) Name and give a general description of your chosen church/cathedral.

(b) Draw and describe one architectural feature from your chosen church/cathedral.

(c) Draw and describe one piece of decoration from your chosen church/cathedral.

Use sketches to illustrate your answer.

exam focus

It is extremely important to include general background information in any answer about Romanesque or Gothic art. Presume your examiner knows nothing at all and give general reasons why churches were built and why this style of sculpture developed, etc. Make sure that any background information you give is relevant to the particular question!

2009 Ordinary Level paper: Section I, Question 8

An example of Romanesque sculpture from the cathedral at Autun is shown below.

Answer (a) and (b)

(a) Describe and discuss this piece of sculpture using the following headings:

- subject matter
- location

(b) Name and describe an example of Romanesque architecture that you have studied.

exam focus

If you have studied architecture, sculpture and stained glass in the Gothic era and can compare the sculpture and architecture to the Romanesque era, you will be well prepared for any question.

Use sketches to illustrate your answer.

2007 Higher Level paper: Section I, Question 8

Romanesque sculpture had decorative and narrative functions.

Discuss this statement in relation to two named examples of Romanesque sculpture you have studied. Emphasise the treatment of the human figure in your answer

and

Name a Romanesque church you have studied and discuss briefly the relationship between its architecture and sculpture.

Illustrate your answer.

2005 Higher Level paper: Section I, Question 8

Answer (a) and (b)

(a) Describe and discuss the characteristics of Gothic sculpture and its relationship to the architecture of the period. Use specific examples.

(b) How does Gothic sculpture differ from the sculpture of the Romanesque period?

Use specific examples.

Illustrate your answer.

2006 Higher Level paper: Section I, Question 8

Discuss, in detail, the stained glass window shown below.

Refer in your answer to its overall plan/design, theme and composition, use of colour and the technique used in its construction

and

Discuss the contribution stained glass windows made to the overall impact of a named Gothic cathedral you have studied.

Illustrate your answer.

2008 Higher Level paper: Section I, Question 8

Describe and discuss the development of Gothic architecture from the twelfth to the sixteenth century, making reference to the **three illustrations** below.

In your answer name the buildings and refer to structure, decoration and style.

Illustrate your answer.

2009 Higher Level paper: Section I, Question 8

During the Gothic period in Europe, the range and style of religious sculpture developed significantly.

Discuss this statement in relation to two named examples of Gothic sculpture you have studied. Emphasise the treatment of the human figure in your answer.

and

Name a Gothic church you have studied and discuss briefly the relationship between its architecture and sculpture.

Use sketches to illustrate your answer.

Extract from the Chief Examiner's Report 2005

Question 8: Gothic Sculpture

This was the second most popular question in Section 2. In their answers, high-scoring candidates displayed a comprehensive familiarity with Gothic sculpture and its relationship with architecture. Specific examples cited included: the cathedrals of Chartres and Notre Dame, Paris; and sculptors Claus Sluter and the Pisanos. Such candidates also displayed a clear understanding of the differences between the two periods and used Autun to underpin the points they made. In the lower attainment range, candidates tended to use stock answers that did not address the specific aspects of the question and/or concentrated solely on Romanesque period.

The International Style

Artists and ideas travelled from one country to another and during the fourteenth century a style evolved which has become known as the 'International Style'.

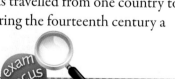

key point

Questions relating to this area come up regularly. It is an easy area to study but make sure you study Painting in Italy to cover it fully.

exam focus

Note this comment from the Chief Examiner's Report 2005 on this section:

Question 9: Choice of Works: This question was answered by few candidates. The most popular choices were The Wilton Diptych and The Virgin and Child window from the Chartres Cathedral. Answers were typified by short discussion of the work and by little mention of style and techniques.

Strive for better answers in your own exam!

The *Wilton Diptych*

- The *Wilton Diptych* can be found in the National Gallery in London.
- It was possibly painted by a French master.
- This is a life-like portrait of Richard II with his patron saints, who recommend him to the Virgin.
- It is a perfect example of delicacy and refinement.

The Wilton Diptych

- Richard is shown kneeling in prayer before the Virgin and her child, who leans towards him playfully.
- The art of the *Wilton Diptych* shows a taste for flowing lines and the delicate and dainty motifs of the art of the time.

Painted books

It was the custom in the Middle Ages to illustrate calendars with the labours of the month. These were attached to prayer books and were called 'Books of Hours'.

Les Très Riches Heures du Duc De Berry

- This is one of the most famous painted books.
- It is a book of prayer, but it is more about the Duc himself.
- The Duc du Berry was a patron of the arts and sought out and encouraged new artists.
- The Limbourg brothers from the Netherlands brought new realism to art.
- This real space and sense of action was a new departure for the miniature painting of France.
- Castles and richly dressed courtiers are all portrayed in precise detail.

September: Les Très Riches Heures du Duc de Berry

- Each month has an illustration:
  - In May the courtiers don leaves and garlands and go riding.
  - In the heat of August they ride out with the falcons while the workers toil in the background, some taking a moment to swim in the river.
  - In September the workers on the estate gather in the grapes in front of the great chateau of Saumur.
  - From March to December each month is depicted with one of the great castles and the estates surrounding them.

Painting in Italy

The Dominican and Franciscan orders were passionate preachers in late Medieval Europe. They preached in the simple language of the people and mingled with them in cities like Florence and Rome.

St Francis and Realism in Art

The founder of the Franciscan order was St Francis of Assisi. He had promoted realistic art as a means of explaining the scriptures to ordinary people, the vast majority of whom could not read. His influence brought a new awareness of the role of the narrative or story in art.

Cimabue and Giotto

The Florentine artist Cimabue was the first to work in this new way. He had a widespread reputation in his time, but today is better known for his pupil Giotto.

Giotto di Bondone

Legend has it that Cimabue found the boy on a hillside drawing sheep on a slate and took him back to Florence. He was apprenticed to Cimabue and learned alongside him in his workshop in Florence. Giotto quickly surpassed his master to become the most famous artist of the time. Giotto's style of painting fell out of favour after his death. His discoveries remained neglected and forgotten until the Renaissance artist Masaccio revived the style.

Giotto's innovations

- He created the illusion of real space.
- He portrayed real people set against real backgrounds almost like a drama on a stage.
- He used correct proportions, foreshortening and light and shade.
- He had an extraordinary ability to convey human emotion through facial expressions and lifelike gestures.
- He improved on traditional fresco techniques. He worked with wet plaster, which bonded with the colour to make it firm and lasting.

Fresco painting

- *Fresco* means fresh in Italian and it is a type of mural painting.
- Giotto was the first painter to change from working with the traditional *a secco* or dry technique to *fresh, buon* or wet plaster.
- Wet plaster gave the artist only a short period of time to work and traditionally a section was completed in a day.

exam focus

A question on Giotto will often ask you to discuss Giotto's development in painting by comparing it to earlier work by Cimabue.

The Madonna Enthroned

- The Madonna Enthroned or *Ognissanti* (all saints) was a particularly popular image. Many artists painted this but the difference between Cimabue's and Giotto's version is very significant.
- Giotto includes traditional symbols but gives the scene real space with depth. He maintains the Virgin's dignified manner but at the same time creates a real woman in a naturalistic pose.

Madonna Enthroned, Cimabue

Ognissanti Madonna, Giotto

The Arena Chapel

- Giotto was employed by a wealthy Paduan merchant called Enrico Scrovegni to decorate the small family chapel.
- Enrico undertook the project of decorating the chapel attached to the Scrovegni Palace to make up for the sins of his father. His father had made his money in banking, but lending money for interest was considered the sin of usury at that time.
- Giotto covered the walls of the small chapel with frescoed scenes from the Life of Jesus.
- The first scenes are dedicated to Mary's life.
- The corrupt influence of money is highlighted in the scene where Jesus chases the moneychangers out of the temple.
- In the Last Judgement scene, Scrovegni himself offers a small model of the chapel to Mary as retribution for his father's wealth.
- Memorable scenes from the Arena Chapel include: The Lament for Christ and The Kiss of Judas.

The Lament for Christ

- Here the figures are lifelike with real expressions of deep human grief.
- Dramatic foreshortening is used to make the gestures more real.
- All the gestures lead the eye to the lifeless figure of Christ.
- Mary Magdalene holds Jesus' feet and gazes at the wounds.
- Mary holds her head close to her son and encloses her arms around him.
- Angels above the group wring their hands in gestures of deep anguish.

The Lament for Christ, Giotto

The Kiss of Judas

- This tense dramatic scene is a powerful image of good versus evil.
- As Judas reaches out to embrace Jesus, his great yellow cloak sweeps forward to cover him.
- The two faces–one serene and dignified, the other evil and repellent–look intently at each other.

The Kiss of Judas, Giotto

2007 Ordinary Level paper: Section II, Question 9

The Kiss of Judas by Giotto (1266–1337).

Answer (a), (b) **and** (c)

(a) Describe and discuss this work under the following headings:

- subject matter
- composition and perspective
- style and medium

(b) How does Giotto convey drama in this work?

(c) Name and give a brief description of another work by Giotto.

Use sketches to illustrate your answer.

2007 Higher Level paper: Section I, Question 9

Describe and discuss *Les Très Riches Heures du Duc de Berry* by the Limbourg brothers, making reference to style, composition, function and the period in which it was produced

and

Name and briefly describe and discuss one other work from this period.

Illustrate your answer.

2009 Higher Level paper: Section I, Question 9

Compare and discuss the *Madonna in Maestà* (Madonna Enthroned with Angels and Prophets) by Cimabue (1240–1302) with *The Kiss of Judas* by Giotto (1267–1337).

Make reference to style, composition, subject matter and the period in which they were produced

and

Name and briefly discuss one work from the International Gothic style.

Use sketches to illustrate your answer.

6 The Renaissance

Rediscovering antiquity

The Renaissance was a period of extraordinary creative and intellectual achievement. It was inspired by the literature, language, culture and art of classical Rome and Greece.

key point

Excellent pictures and information on Renaissance artists can be found on www.wga.hu.

- The word 'Renaissance' means rebirth in French and is today mostly associated with the visual arts.

- A new philosophy called humanism became widespread among intellectuals. This philosophy valued human achievements because man was God's creation.

exam focus

Questions in this section may not ask for an artist by name, so make sure you understand their areas of speciality.

Make sure that you are familiar with artists and artworks from the early and high Renaissance.

Learn painting, sculpture and architecture and make sure you understand the influence of one on the other.

- The ancient worlds of Greece and Rome were considered the highest point of human intellectual achievement.

- Beauty was also highly regarded as a way towards God.

- Printing helped to spread the new ideas from humanist literature as well as translations from classical works about science and astronomy.

- The growth of European cities contributed greatly to the spread of learning. The main centres of wealth, education and culture were London, Amsterdam, Paris, Vienna, Venice and Florence.

Florence

The Republic of Florence was a small independent city state. One of the most powerful and prosperous in Europe, it had a strong woollen industry and its own currency–a gold coin called the florin. This was an important trade coin of Western Europe.

As well as being a thriving commercial centre, Florence was a place that showed high regard for all things cultural and intellectual. Humanist scholars found it easy to promote the notion of the dignity and importance of man.

The Baptistery Doors in Florence

The Trade Guilds

- The guilds were major patrons of art in Renaissance Florence.
- These associations of master craftsmen set standards of apprenticeship, qualification and good workmanship.
- They were extremely powerful politically and virtually controlled the city's government.
- Some were very wealthy and took financial responsibility for the city's major churches, hospitals and charitable institutions.
- Examples of guilds include: the Arte de **Cambrio**, the guild of the bankers; and the Arte dei Mercanti di **Calimala**, the guild of the wool and cloth merchants.

> **key point**
>
> The construction of Florence Cathedral took over a century. A series of competitions were held at several stages of its completion. These competitions became one of the main driving forces of artistic development in the city.

The Baptistery

- The Cathedral and the Baptistery were the responsibility of the Calimala guild.
- The Baptistery was dedicated to the patron saint of Florence, St John the Baptist.
- The Calimala restored the building around A.D. 1200, covering it with green and white marble cladding.
- In the late thirteenth century they replaced the wooden entrance doors and commissioned the sculptor Andrea Pisano to make new bronze doors.

> **key point**
>
> Visit www.sacred-destinations.com for a short history of Florence and some detailed pictures of the Baptistery.

The first Baptistery Doors: Andrea Pisano

- These doors were made of bronze with gilded (thinly layered gold) figures.
- Twenty-eight relief scenes from the life and death of St John the Baptist were featured.
- Each scene was enclosed within a *quatrefoil* (four arcs placed together).
- Scenes relate to the theme of baptism.

The competition for the second Baptistery Doors

- The fifteenth century in Florence began with one of the most famous competitions in the history of art.
- The Calimala celebrated the year 1400 with a competition to design a new set of doors for the Baptistery.
- The brief was to design doors to match the style of Andrea Pisano's for the main doors facing the Cathedral.
- Artists had to submit a trial piece. The rules were strict:

- It had to be a gilded relief sculpture.
- The subject was The Sacrifice of Isaac.
- The details of the story had to be exactly right.
- It had to maintain the same quatrefoil shape as Andrea Pisano's panels.
- Twenty-three-year-old Filippo Brunelleschi and twenty-year-old Lorenzo Ghiberti were declared joint winners.
- Brunelleschi was bitterly disappointed and left Florence, while Ghiberti worked on the Baptistery doors for the rest of his life.

The second Baptistery Doors: Lorenzo Ghiberti

Baptistery Doors, Lorenzo Ghiberti

- The subject of the new doors was the 'Life of Christ'.
- It took Ghiberti twenty-seven years to complete them.
- He made a great deal of artistic progress over the years.
- These 28 panels are fuller and more adventurous than Pisano's earlier work.
- Brunelleschi had by now developed the technique of perspective and this influenced Ghiberti in his work.
- An interesting scene in the Baptistery Doors is that of *The Flagellation of Christ.* This shows the classical spirit of the Renaissance: Jesus appears in a gently curved pose, set against classical Corinthian columns.

The third Baptistery Doors: Lorenzo Ghiberti

When the doors were complete, the Calimala immediately agreed a further contract with Ghiberti for a third set. Ghiberti was an architect and master craftsman by now. This meant that he could make decisions on the design of the work himself.

East side Baptistery Doors

- Ghiberti cut the number of panels to ten and introduced an entirely new framing system. This decision was influenced by the work of Donatello, a contemporary sculptor.
- Overall, the doors have a more unified appearance with more space for the stories.
- The subject matter is the Old Testament. Several episodes of the one story appear in each panel. They include perspective and three-dimensional figures.

- *The Story of Jacob and Esau* features in the Baptistery Doors. In this Bible story, Esau loses his birthright to his brother Jacob. The old man Isaac mistakenly blesses his second son with the help of his wife. In Ghiberti's depiction of this story, single point perspective leads the eye to the central architectural arch and the various groups of figures involved in the story.

The Story of Jacob and Esau panel from the east doors of the Baptistery.

Art takes priority

- When the doors were finished in 1452 the Calimala made an extraordinary decision. They were so impressed by their splendour that they moved Ghiberti's earlier set to the north door. The new golden doors were now facing the Cathedral.

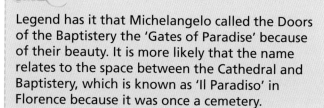

key point

Legend has it that Michelangelo called the Doors of the Baptistery the 'Gates of Paradise' because of their beauty. It is more likely that the name relates to the space between the Cathedral and Baptistery, which is known as 'Il Paradiso' in Florence because it was once a cemetery.

- Placing Old Testament imagery in front of the Cathedral was a major change in attitude. For the first time art (not its subject) was most important.

Relief sculpture

During the time of his work on the Baptistery Doors, Ghiberti came under the influence of other artists.

key point

This form of low-relief sculpture was called *rilievo schiacciato* meaning 'squashed' or 'flattened relief'.

- Donatello (one of his former students) had become the most prominent sculptor in Florence.

- His old rival Brunelleschi had worked out a method of perspective called 'single point' perspective.
- Donatello was the first artist to use perspective in a relief sculpture. This can be seen in a panel below the statue of St George in the centre of Florence.

The Feast of Herod: Donatello

Donatello's first relief in bronze was a scene from the life of John the Baptist on one of six panels on the base of the Baptismal font in Siena.

- This depicts King Herod's birthday feast.
- He has asked the beautiful princess Salome to dance for him.
- She agrees, but only if he can give her the head of the John the Baptist on a platter.
- Herod recoils in horror when the severed head arrives before him.
- It is a highly emotional scene.

- Several episodes of the story are set in a complex set of spaces going back through the arches.
- Here we see very clever use of perspective.

The free-standing figure

In the early years of the fifteenth century a radically new and very public type of sculpture appeared in Florence. This was before any similar changes had happened in painting or architecture.

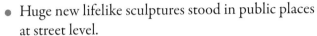

The Feast of Herod, Donatello

- Huge new lifelike sculptures stood in public places at street level.
- Traditional belief was that 'that sculpture hovers somewhere between flesh and stone'.
- People saw them as 'breathing statues in which only the voice is lacking'.

Orsanmichele

- The Church of Orsanmichele was a former grain store made into a church.
- All the guilds in Florence were invited to put a statue of its patron saint in niches around the exterior walls of the church.
- The *Arte del Calimala* (Wool and Cloth Merchants' Guild) chose Lorenzo Ghiberti to create their patron saint of John the Baptist.
- The Linen Workers' Guild commissioned the young and lesser known artist Donatello to carve a statue of St Mark, their patron saint.
- In contrast to Ghiberti's work, St Mark has a very lifelike pose and a real human expression. St Mark's weight is placed over the right leg and the upper body and head are turned in *contrapposto*.
- Shortly afterwards the Armourers' Guild chose Donatello to sculpt St George.

key point

Contrapposto is an Italian word that means 'contrasting poses'. The weight is on one leg and the other is relaxed. The figure's hips and shoulders rest at opposite angles and this tilts the body from hip to shoulder giving a slight s-curve to the entire torso. It was developed by classical Greek sculptors to avoid stiffness.

Donatello (1386–1466)

Donato di Bardi (better known as Donatello) became the most important sculptor in Florence. His work completely changed the approach to sculpture for generations to come.

Classical influence

- Donatello greatly admired classical works of ancient Greece and Rome.
- He used live models for his studies of the human figure.

- He trained in Ghiberti's studio but worked closely with Filippo Brunelleschi, learning the rules of proportion and perspective.
- He spent some time in Rome with him studying antiquities. This influenced him above all and helped to develop his own unique style of art.

Important works

St George

St George, Donatello

- The statue of *St George* made for Orsanmichele is full of strength and courage.
- His hand resting on his shield is firm and his gaze is fixed and strong.
- This warrior knight in classical armour is a convincingly real person standing with feet resolutely apart.
- The tense but determined face is a study of concentrated energy.

David

- This is one of the most important sculptures of the early Renaissance.
- Donatello was also the first artist since Classical times to produce a life-sized, fully three-dimensional nude figure.
- *David* is made of bronze and is nude apart from his hat and leggings.
- The s-shape is similar to classical statues but this slim adolescent boy is quite unlike the powerful Greek gods of antiquity. Instead he presents an image of youth that is pure and incorrupt.
- A highly polished bronze surface is used on the areas of smooth skin and this contrasts a rougher finish for the hair and hat.

David, Donatello

Mary Magdalen

- Donatello's *Mary Magdalen* is the most famous of his late works.
- This tragic figure in painted wood is surely the most haunting and represents a timeless image of all human suffering.
- Sad blue eyes stare from hollow sockets and the half open mouth shows broken white teeth.
- Bones protrude from gaunt cheeks and the yellow streaked hair is matted and twisted in tangled curves.
- In a gesture of penitence one knee is slightly bent, but the long veined feet still have a suggestion of youthful beauty.

Mary Magdalen, Donatello

- The figure has real presence and power to touch the emotions of the viewer.

Learn by drawing!
One of the best ways to study these three key works by Donatello is to draw them yourself.

Donatello regularly comes up on exam papers. Have a good understanding of his important role. St George, David and Mary Magdalene are his most famous works, but also mention the influence of The Feast of Herod in your answer.

Patronage in fifteenth-century Italy

- The Italian peninsula was a series of independent states ruled by dukes and princes. Milan was one of the largest and most important of these, but Mantua and Urbino had important courts that spent money lavishly on culture and art.
- Venice, Sienna and Florence were small city states. Although they were surrounded by enemies, they remained strong and independent.

The primary purpose of religious art was to glorify God but it also enhanced the status of the patron and his family. The patron's taste was reflected in the artist's style.

- Rulers had traditionally been patrons of art but the new humanist way of thinking gave this even more emphasis. It was important for rulers to be seen to spend generously on fine buildings and works of art.
- Renaissance Florence was a major centre of artistic activities. As well as the guilds, there were many private patrons and they commissioned works of art that were mainly religious.

The Medici family

The family best known for its artistic patronage was the Medici family: Cosimo, his son Piero and his grandson Lorenzo. Florence was a republic but the Medici family managed to get into a position where they alone ruled Florence. Florence prospered under the Medici and the arts flourished.

- Cosimo de Medici was a humanist but was deeply religious. He spent a good deal of money on the construction, restoration and decoration of church sites.

Scene from the *Procession of the Magi*, Gozzolio

- Cosimo's son Piero died quite young, so his grandson Lorenzo took over the rule of Florence at just twenty-one years old. He has become better known as Lorenzo the Magnificent.
- The Medici employed many well-known artists. Amongst the earliest were Fra Angelico and Paulo Ucello.

Fra Angelico and the Convent of San Marco

- One of the buildings restored by Cosimo was the Dominican Monastery or Convent of San Marco.
- He chose one of the monks called Fra Giovanni to paint the walls with frescoes. He has become better known as Fra Angelico.
- Fra Angelico and his assistants painted a sacred scene at the end of every corridor and in each monk's cell. *The Annunciation* is the best-known of these.

Main altarpiece of the Chapel at San Marco

- Cosimo de Medici also commissioned an altarpiece for the high altar in the church of San Marco dedicated to Saints Cosmos and Damian.
- When the altarpiece was taken apart later, the nine small pictures in the *predella* (the base) were removed.
- One of these pictures is in the National Gallery Dublin. The scene shows the attempted martyrdom by fire of Saints Cosmos and Damien along with three of their brothers.
- In the scene, the flames have spread outwards miraculously and have forced the executioners to flee, leaving the saints untouched.
- This small work was carefully planned to create a very clever illusion of space and depth.

Paulo Uccello (1397–1475)

Paulo Uccello was highly regarded in his own time. He became obsessed by mathematical principles in painting. He made three panels for Cosimo de Medici depicting the Battle of San Romano. This was a victory for Florence but was an event of little or no importance. It would have been quickly forgotten but for Uccello's paintings.

The Battle of San Romano, Uccello

The Battle of San Romano Panels

- The panels originally decorated the large hall on the ground floor of the Medici Palace but one is now in the Louvre in Paris, one in the Uffizi Gallery in Florence and one in the National Gallery, London.
- The panels indicate both the artist's and the patron's fascination with details and weapons of war.
- The painting in London features General Niccolò da Tolentino, who seems to have been a friend of Cosimo de Medici.

- General Niccolò da Tolentino was a mercenary soldier and in the painting he is completely idealised. He wears his ceremonial outfit and sits on his lovely white horse, appearing unaffected by the battle.
- The painting clearly shows Uccello's preoccupation with single point perspective and foreshortening. This can be seen in the shapes, broken lances, posture and proportions of the horses and the fallen soldier in the foreground.

The Brancacci Chapel

The Brancacci were another of Florence's rich and powerful banking families. They commissioned a work of art for their private chapel at the side of the church of St Maria del Carmine. This was to be a source of inspiration for artists for over a century.

The artists

- The artist was the well-established painter Masolino da Panicale.
- His young assistant Masaccio joined him and they frescoed the panels of the upper walls until Masolino left to work elsewhere.
- Masaccio continued the work on the lower panels until his early death at twenty-seven years old.

Masaccio (1401–28)

- Masaccio was a remarkable painter and he created some of the most monumental works of the early Renaissance.
- His classical style was restrained, exact, scientific and highly innovative.

key point

Masaccio was the first artist to revive Giotto's innovations of over a hundred years before.

It is important to study Giotto's paintings in order to fully appreciate Masaccio's work.

The Brancacci Chapel Frescoes

The paintings in the Brancacci Chapel are based on episodes from the life of St Peter but overall represent the story of the salvation.

- It begins with Adam and Eve because their sin against God was the first need for mediation between God and man.
- Masolino and Masaccio each painted Adam and Eve on the entrance columns of the chapel opposite each other.
- Masolino's *Temptation of Adam* is painted in the elegant courtly style.
- Masaccio's *Expulsion from the Garden of Eden* is much more in early Renaissance style.
- The figures are dramatically expressive as they stumble forward in misery and nakedness.
- Their sorrow is concentrated in their gestures and faces. Eve lifts her head to cry out in anguish and Adam covers his face stumbling forward as he weeps bitter tears of shame and regret.
- Eve's gesture is similar to a classical statue called *Venus Pudica* because of how she attempts to cover her nakedness with her hands.

- However, Masaccio's work is not simply a copy of ancient forms. Its fresh realism makes it special and new.

key point

In one section of *The Expulsion from the Garden of Eden*, around Adam's head, blue azurite applied to the dry plaster has completely faded and only the grey-blue primer undercolour applied to the wet plaster has remained. The outline is evidence of a giornata or one day's work in fresco.

The Expulsion from the Garden of Eden, Masaccio

The Tribute Money, Brancacci Chapel

- This huge scene on the upper level of the chapel relates to the yearly tax payment for the maintenance of the Temple in Jerusalem.

- Jesus and his disciples have come to the gates of the city and the tax collector asks Peter for money. Peter is reluctant but Jesus insists on payment.

- It is a small and unimportant biblical event and so was an unusual choice for such a large art work.

- It has been interpreted over the years in several ways but the Brancacci family were bankers so it probably relates to the duty to pay taxes.

- The story has three separate moments within the one scene:

key point

Masaccio was greatly influenced by Giotto. Like the older artist, Masaccio created real three-dimensional space and solid sculptural realistic figures with naturalistic expressions and gestures. His work caused a sensation in its own time.

The Tribute Money, Masaccio

  - The centre focuses on Christ pointing towards the left where Peter hesitates. He directs Peter to the lake to get a coin from the fish's mouth.
  - The second episode shows Peter crouched at the lakeside.
  - In the third scene Peter gives the coin to the tax collector at the gate.

- Masaccio shows strong monumental figures painted with sculptural-like shadow.

- Peter's pose is an exact replica of Christ's. Similarly both appearances of the tax collector are mirror images of each other.

- This has the effect of locking the main characters of the story into a single unit within the composition.

- Architectural perspective lines frame the characters and take the eye straight to the face of the central figure of Christ.

The Trinity

- Masaccio's use of perspective can be seen in another famous fresco in Florence. In *The Trinity*, in the church of St Maria Novella, all the lines of perspective converge to a single vanishing point at eye level.
- The painting creates the image of the real space of a small chapel with the three persons of the Trinity.
- A huge figure of God the Father supporting the arms of the cross dominates the scene.
- Below the base of the cross and below our line of vision a tomb with a skeleton tilts forward. Written in Latin is an ancient warning that translates: 'I was what you are and what I am you shall be.'

The Trinity, St Maria Novella, Florence

Architecture

The Dome of the Cathedral of St Maria del Fiore in Florence

Filippo Brunelleschi left Florence after the competition for the Doors of the Baptistery. In 1418 he returned, this time to win another equally important competition. This was to design a dome for the Cathedral of St Maria del Fiore. The construction of such a large dome was a problem but Brunelleschi submitted a new and very innovative solution. He also produced a model and he was awarded the commission.

key point

Visit www.sacred-destinations.com to read a short history of the Cathedral of St Maria del Fiore in Florence.

The Dome of St Maria del Fiore, Florence

Filippo Brunelleschi (1377–1446)

- Brunelleschi studied art and design, including mechanics. He began in a goldsmith's workshop but went on to become an architect as well as a sculptor, painter and scholar.
- He developed the laws of perspective.
- He also learned a great deal from the buildings of ancient Rome and his studies of the Pantheon helped with his design for the Dome.

The Dome

- Brunelleschi's design for the dome was unique and technically brilliant.
- It was a self-supporting cupola that had no wooden scaffolding.
- His design was a double shell cupola that included a walkway and steps between the walls.

- Massive stone ribs held the inner and outer shells together.
- Stone chains were buried within the masonry and these strengthened each of the eight faces.
- His expertise at mathematics and geometry and his knowledge of mechanics greatly helped in his plan.
- The brickwork of the walls was in a herring-bone pattern. This meant each ring would be supported by the one below and so the Dome could not collapse in on itself.

The Lantern

- Brunelleschi won another competition to design the lantern on top of the Dome but he did not live to see it in place.
- The lantern has Classical as well as novel architectural features.

Leone Battista Alberti

- Leone Battista Alberti was a member of a wealthy banking family that had been exiled from Florence.
- He spent some time at the Papal Court but then returned to Florence.
- He was so impressed by all the artistic activity that he wrote a book about it. This was the first Renaissance book about art.

Alberti's books

- Alberti wrote two major works: *On Painting* argues the importance of painting as a basis for architecture. *On Architecture* was subdivided into ten books. The books detailed for architects exactly how buildings should be built. These books remained the most important reference books on architecture until the eighteenth century.
- Alberti was an expert humanist and his books put forward new and revolutionary theories. *On Painting* suggested that artists should be recognised as intellectuals and their position in society be stronger.
- *On Architecture* put forth the notion of a well-planned city. Alberti's city designs involved all classes of people living in harmony and elegance around state buildings, temples and palaces. In Alberti's work we can see the influence of the ancient Roman architect Vitruvius and his classical buildings.
- Alberti became an architect and, like Brunelleschi, his new classical style became extremely popular in Italy.

The 'Golden Age' of the Renaissance in Florence

Lorenzo the Magnificent

- Lorenzo de Medici took over as ruler of Florence at the age of twenty-one, after his father's early death. He was a skilled politician as well as a poet and a generous patron of the arts.

- Lorenzo's time as ruler became known as the 'Golden Age' of the Florentine Renaissance and he earned the title 'Lorenzo the Magnificent'.

Botticelli (1445–1510)

- The young artist Sandro Botticelli came to live in the Medici Palace when Lorenzo and his brother Giuliano were young. They became friends and shared an interest in humanist literature and philosophy.
- Botticelli's artworks have become the most recognised works of the Florentine Renaissance.
- He trained in the workshop of Fra Filippo Lippi and learned to paint an idealised, slightly melancholic image of feminine beauty.
- Botticelli's painting of the *Adoration of the Magi* includes portraits of Medici family members.
- He worked with the Medici family and was influenced by Lorenzo's intellectual friends.
- He was introduced to classical poetry and he painted mythological themes related to it.
- His most famous paintings, *Primavera* and *The Birth of Venus,* hung in the Medici Palace for many years.

Neoplatonism

- Botticelli's *Primavera* is one of the most famous paintings of the Renaissance, but it is quite controversial to this day.
- It was painted for a member of a humanist group known as the Neoplatonists.
- Neoplatonists greatly admired the Greek philosopher Plato. They believed in a hidden agreement between Christianity and pagan mythology.
- The painting's true meaning may have been suppressed for religious reasons.

Primavera (The Coming of Spring)

- All the figures in this painting are from the classical world.
- Venus, the goddess of beauty, celebrates the arrival of Spring but her expression of melancholy purity is like that of Botticelli's religious figures.
- The women are pregnant, symbolising fertility.

Primavera, Botticelli

- The painting 'reads' from right to left. It begins with Zephyr, the wind, pursuing Chloris, the wood nymph, with flowers falling from her mouth.
- Chloris transforms into Flora, scattering blossoms before her.

- Cupid, the blindfold son of Venus, shoots his arrow towards the girls dancing in an endless circle of life.
- Mercury, the messenger of the gods, holds up his staff to remove the cloud that hides the truth.

The Birth of Venus

The Birth of Venus, Botticelli

- *The Birth of Venus* was painted as a wedding present for a member of the Medici family.
- It was quite unlike other paintings of the time and was kept hidden for many years.
- The subject of Venus coming in from the sea on a shell was well known from a classical poem.
- In Botticelli's picture, the figure of Venus is elongated. She has a very long neck and sharply sloping shoulders, but she is the very image of graceful elegance with hair blowing in the wind.
- Her pose is similar to the classical statue of Venus Pudica.
- Venus is considered to have one of the most beautiful faces in art.
- Botticelli used the same model for some of his religious paintings.

A Linear Artist

- Botticelli painted almost entirely with line.
- He used little or no light and shade.
- He also kept his painted surfaces very simple. This can be seen in *The Birth of Venus*, where the waves on the sea are shown with a series of little v's.

Savanarola

- In later life Botticelli became a follower of the monk Savonarola, who preached against the corrupt lifestyle of the city and the 'paganism' of the Medici.
- In a frenzy of religious intensity Botticelli began to fear for his salvation.
- He became deeply religious, destroyed some of his earlier paintings and produced only religious works for the rest of his life.
- Botticelli fell out of favour with his patrons and was forgotten after he died.
- It was the nineteenth century before his painting became popular again.

Urbino

Another of Italy's famous centres of art was the little Duchy of Urbino. Its court was famous for its great cultural and artistic activity. This was mainly due to its ruler Duke Federigo da Montefeltro.

- Urbino was in a very isolated position in the mountains so the Duke had to search widely for artists.

- He had many contacts due to his former career as a military captain and diplomat.
- His artists reflected his refined taste and his main focus was his Ducal Palace.
- He was influenced by Cosimo de Medici's palace in Florence.
- He also followed the guidelines of the humanist scholar Leone Alberti's book, *On Architecture*.

A Renaissance Man

- Federigo da Montefeltro set a very high standard of leadership and Urbino became renowned as a centre of learning.
- He was deeply religious but had great interest in philosophy, Latin and Greek, as well as mathematics.
- His young wife was Battista Sforza of Milan, who was also highly regarded for her intelligence. She died at the age of twenty-five, shortly after the birth of her son. The Duke greatly mourned her loss.

Piero della Francesca (1415–1492)

- One of the artists brought to Urbino by the Duke was Piero della Francesca. He shared many of his patron's intellectual interests and he too was particularly keen on mathematics.
- Piero della Francesca was all but forgotten for many years. He is regarded as one of the greatest of all Italian painters, but his lack of popularity may have related to his austere, intellectual style of painting.
- He worked in small, little-known towns but absorbed a good deal of the artistic discoveries of his predecessors and contemporaries in Florence.

Federigo da Montefeltro, Duke of Urbino, and his wife, Battista Sforza

- Piero painted the famous double portrait of Federigo da Montefeltro and his wife Battista Sforza.
- They are shown in profile probably because the Duke's face was badly disfigured during a jousting tournament.
- It was also in keeping with the new art of portraiture that imitated the medals of ancient Rome.
- It was however highly unusual to place the couple facing each other in this way.
- It suggests a sad and never-ending partnership.

Federigo da Montefeltro, Duke of Urbino, and his wife, Battista Sforza, Piero della Francesca

The Baptism of Christ

- *The Baptism of Christ* is one of Piero's early paintings.
- It was painted for a church in his native town of Sansepolcro.

- The figures show the grace and serenity for which he was famous.
- Gentle coloured light and delicate colours combine with perfect perspective to convey a deeply spiritual atmosphere.
- The sky is mirrored in the still water as the Holy Spirit hovers over St John.
- Fine lines of gold suggest heavenly light falling on Christ's head.
- Piero was a significant influence on later painters. One of these was Perugino, whose own pupil was Raphael, the great master of the High Renaissance.

Baptism of Christ by Piero della Francesca, (c.1415–92)

The Early Renaissance in the North

Religious painting

- In the early fifteenth century another important movement in painting was taking place in Flanders.
- This area of northern Europe is Belgium and part of France today but at that time it was all part of the Duchy of Burgundy.
- The cities of Ghent and Bruges were very prosperous and there was a strong demand for religious painting.
- Artists were concerned with realistic space and the human figure, but there was no humanist influence.
- The depiction of naturalism was therefore very different from that seen in Florence.

Flemish painting

- Flemish paintings appear medieval in style when compared to Italian Renaissance painting. Figures have solemn facial features and awkward figure postures.
- Sacred scenes were often placed in ordinary domestic interiors.
- Perspective was less advanced than in Italy, so space often appeared distorted.
- Despite this, Italian artists were very influenced by northern artists. They greatly admired their careful observation of nature and portrayal of detail in shiny metal, glass, fur and velvet.

Oil painting

- Flemish artists used oil paint. They mixed traditional paint pigment with oil instead of water.
- This was used on wood panels because fresco on walls was not suitable in the damp climate.

- Layers of thin oily paint had a tinted, translucent look.
- The mixture dried slowly, allowing the artist to blend the colours and make changes more easily.
- The artist had more freedom to depict fine detail.
- The mixture dried to a hard, opaque, enamel-like finish.
- This gave it a smooth, shiny, velvety surface, unlike the quick-drying egg tempera used in Italy that often had a dry and powdery look.

Jan van Eyck (circa 1390 –1441)

- Jan van Eyck was one of the main founders of the Flemish school. Van Eyck was painting in Ghent at the same time as Masaccio was working in Florence.
- Van Eyck developed oil painting to a very high level of refinement and skill.
- He also developed 'atmospheric perspective', which means colours and shapes blur in the atmosphere of distant landscape.
- Van Eyck painted microscopic detail with an amazingly high degree of realism.

Madonna with the Chancellor Rolin

- This painting features Nicholas Rolin who was the Chancellor of Burgundy in 1422.
- It shows him kneeling in piety and silent meditation in his magnificent palace.
- He looks up from his prayers to see the Queen of Heaven crowned by an angel and the infant raising his hand in blessing.
- Details of the room and the chancellor's fine velvet robes are particularly beautifully depicted.
- Through the window a panoramic view is seen stretching into the distance past the town towards the hills.

Giovanni Arnolfini and His Wife

- This is the most famous of Van Eyck's paintings.
- It shows the commercial connection between Italy and Burgundy. It features the Italian merchant Giovanni Arnolfini and his fiancée Giovanna Cenami of Bruges.
- The painting celebrates the couple's betrothal. They wear elaborate ceremonial costumes and hold hands solemnly.
- All the elements of the room and the clothing are painted in minute detail.

Giovanni Arnolfini and His Wife,
Jan van Eyck

Giovanni Arnolfini and His Wife is one of the best-known paintings in the world and is therefore likely to come up in an exam question from time to time.

- The painting is full of symbolic detail:
  - The shoes on the floor indicate a holy place for sacred ceremony.
  - The dog represents faithfulness in marriage.
  - The fruit on the window is man's innocence in the Garden of Eden.
  - The crystal beads and the spotless mirror indicate Mary's purity.
  - One candle burning denotes the presence of Christ but also signifies the taking of an oath.
  - The peculiar stance of the bride suggests pregnancy or may represent the possibility of children in the future.

> **key point**
>
> This was the first full-length painting of real people in a real life event. It gave portraiture a new and more important position.

- The mirror on the wall is a remarkable piece of miniature painting. In it, the figures are reversed and the painter is facing them.
- This suggests that the artist is a witness at the ceremony. His name also appears on the wall above, written in the formal decorative handwriting associated with legal documents.
- The Latin translates: 'Jan van Eyck was here 1434'.

The High Renaissance: Rome and Florence

The High Renaissance, as it has become known, was a golden age in its own time. Florence was the source of the inspiration but the movement soon spread to Rome. The economy of Rome had been poor but two Popes set out to change this. Pope Julius II and later Pope Leo X, son of Lorenzo de Medici, wanted the city returned to its ancient position of cultural and political glory. They employed some of the leading artists and craftsmen of the time. They spent a great deal of money and this resulted in some of the world's most treasured works of art. The rebuilding of St Peter's Basilica began at this time.

Innovations in painting

The changes that took place in painting at this time were:

- More realism in figures.
- More lifelike facial features and expressions.
- A greater range of human movement.
- Figures that related to each other in a more natural manner within the compositions.

Craftsman to genius

During the High Renaissance the attitude towards artists changed greatly.

- Leone Battista Alberti and Leonardo da Vinci both wrote books that were very influential in changing the artist's professional and social status.
- Painting was now on a par with other complex intellectual activities.

- Traditionally artists had been considered mere craftsmen, but now successful artists were expected to be well educated.
- Their opinions were respected and they shared their thoughts with other intellectual, educated people, including their patrons.
- The status of the artist changed radically to the notion of the artist as very special and perhaps even a genius.

key point

Draw two works each by Leonardo, Michelangelo and Raphael in detail. Then learn about the artists and the ideals of the High Renaissance.

key point

Remember that Michelangelo was a sculptor, painter and architect!

High Renaissance artists

- Leonardo da Vinci, Michelangelo and Raphael were regarded as geniuses in their own time.
- This gave them freedom to pick and choose work.
- Patrons were honoured to have such a high-profile artist work for them.
- They tolerated Leonardo's habit of leaving work unfinished.
- Michelangelo was allowed to argue with the Pope.
- Raphael was said to have followers like that of a prince.

Leonardo da Vinci (1452–1519)

Leonardo da Vinci was the oldest and most famous of the great Renaissance masters.

He is regarded as the ultimate Renaissance man because of his wide-ranging talents.

He had interests from natural science, engineering and architecture to philosophy and art.

He designed buildings, drainage systems, weapons of war and a flying machine!

Early life
- Leonardo came from the little town of Vinci in the Tuscan hills.
- He was apprenticed to the painter and sculptor Andrea del Verrocchio in Florence.
- He moved to Milan to work in the court of Ludovico Sforza.

Milan
- The city-state of Milan was wealthy and powerful.
- Its rulers were the Sforza family and they paid for the rebuilding of the church of Sante Maria delle Grazie.
- It was here that Leonardo painted his famous fresco of the Last Supper.

The Last Supper
- Many artists had painted this scene before, but Leonardo's version is very special.
- In the picture he uses natural gestures and facial expressions.
- It tells the story in a silent yet highly dramatic way.
- Leonardo chose the moment when Jesus said: 'One of you will betray me.'

- He shows the apostles reeling in horror. Each one has a particular expression of confusion, denial or disbelief.
- They are arranged in groups, with some drawing away from Christ and others leaning towards him.
- The central figure of Jesus remains serene and dignified.

The Last Supper, Leonardo da Vinci

- The picture uses clever perspective to suggest a wall receding back. All the perspective lines lead to the central figure of Christ.
- *The Last Supper* is unfortunately in semi-ruined state.
- Leonardo was frustrated with the fast-drying fresco. This prevented him from using the kind of fine detail he liked.
- He therefore experimented and used oil mixed with the tempera paint.
- This caused problems and within twenty years it began to disintegrate.
- Since that time every generation has worked hard to preserve the artwork.

Scientific interests

- Leonardo recorded his studies of mathematics, geology, the human body and other scientific subjects in his manuscripts.
- He studied anatomy and dissected dead bodies to understand the workings of bones and muscles and the position of the baby in the womb.
- He also made hundreds of drawings of places, people and plants. He made interesting studies of animals, particularly horses.
- He was also interested in atmospheric elements, like rain and dust. He studied their effect on colour.
- He studied perspective and was one the first Italian artists to use atmospheric perspective.

The Virgin of the Rocks

- This painting shows Leonardo's interest in and close observation of nature.
- It is seen in the plants and flowers as well the strange landscapes of water and rock formations in the background.
- There are two versions of this painting: one is in the Louvre and a later version is in The National Gallery, London.
- The Virgin and child with St John are placed in an imaginary enchanted grotto.
- The paintings show Leonardo's love of the mysterious.

The Virgin of the Rocks, Leonardo da Vinci

Sfumato

- Leonardo had a huge interest in light and shade and he developed a technique called *sfumato* (the Italian word for smoke).
- This softens outlines allowing a smooth passage from light to shade. It is seen to great effect on faces both in his religious works and his portraits.

key point

Try a Google search on the word *sfumato* and choose web definitions. The results could be very interesting.

Portraits

Leonardo painted many portraits of women.

Ginevra de Benci

- *Ginevra de Benci* is an early work.
- Ginevra is placed in a calm, three-quarters pose.
- She looks directly at the viewer and has the sad and mysterious beauty typical of Leonardo's work.

Lady with an Ermine

- *Lady with an Ermine* is a portrait of Cecilia Gallerani, a prominent lady at the court of Milan.
- A mistress of the Duke, she was known not just for her beauty but also as a poetess and lover of Latin.
- The ermine is pun on Cecilia's surname and the Greek word for ermine, which is *galen*.
- Instead of a conventional pose, Cecelia is turned to the left. This displays the elegant line of her throat and curved shoulders.
- Her long, tapering fingers are typical of Leonardo's work.
- The painting became instantly famous and became the new ideal for elegant female portraiture.

Mona Lisa

- Leonardo's most famous portrait is the *Mona Lisa*.
- Here the artist has combined *sfumato* with *chiaroscuro* (the balance of light against dark).
- There have been many interpretations about the work for many years.
- The skilful brushwork and realistic depiction of flesh and clothing continue to fascinate visitors to the Louvre in Paris, but this portrait remains as mysterious as it ever was.
- The painting is in poor condition because once again Leonardo experimented with media. This makes it very difficult to restore.

Mona Lisa, Leonardo da Vinci

Later life

- Leonardo had to get out of Milan when it was invaded by French troops in 1500.
- He returned to Florence briefly and even went to Rome in the hope of getting commissions from the newly elected Pope Leo X.
- However, the Pope was more interested in Raphael Sanzio, a young artist from Urbino, and Leonardo's old rival from Florence, the great Michelangelo Buonarroti.
- Leonardo's work was seen as anti-Christian, so in the end he was forced to leave Italy. He found refuge in the court of the King of France, where he died in 1519.

Michelangelo Buonarroti (1475–1564)

Early life

- Michelangelo spent a short time in the studio of the artist Ghirlandaio as a boy.
- He first came to notice when he was seventeen years old. He was by then living in the Palazzo Medici under the protection and financial support of Lorenzo the Magnificent.
- Here he studied from the Medici collection of classical statues.
- He also spent many months copying from Masaccio's frescoes in the Brancacci Chapel.
- After Lorenzo's death, Michelangelo left Florence to find new patrons
- At twenty-three years of age he produced one of his most beautiful works for the tomb of an elderly French cardinal in Rome. This firmly established his name.

Sculpture

Pietà

- The theme of the *pietà* was quite common in northern art but Michelangelo presented the subject in an entirely new manner.
- The word *pietà* in religious art always refers to the Virgin grieving over the dead Christ.
- This was a theme that Michelangelo returned to several times in his life but the first is probably the most beautiful, elegant and harmonious of all.
- It is the only work he ever signed.
- The young Madonna is dignified and calm. The sad event is presented in a restrained and classical manner.
- The figures are completely realistic but are idealised beyond the mere human to the divine.
- Michelangelo solved the technical problem of laying a grown man on the lap of a seated woman by building up the drapery to form in a pyramid of support with the cloth.

Pietà, Michelangelo

The Republic as Patron

- The young artist returned to Florence in 1500 to undertake a commission for the *Signoria* (governors).
- Florence was a republic again and to celebrate Michelangelo was asked to make a statue for the cathedral.
- He was given a gigantic block of marble and with it he produced the great statue of David.

David

David, Michelangelo

- *David* is four meters high,
- This young boy who killed the huge Goliath with one shot from his sling symbolises the strength of Florence against its stronger enemies.
- The face has a determined frown but this is a classical statue. It is extremely realistic but idealised to a divine level.
- This perfectly proportioned and flawlessly beautiful male is like one of the classical statues of the Gods of antiquity.
- There is a resemblance to Venus in Botticelli's *Birth of Venus*, in terms of pose and gesture.
- The statue was completed in one year.
- The Signoria of Florence were so impressed that instead of placing it on the cathedral it was put it in the main Piazza of Florence.

A tomb for Pope Julius

- Soon after this, the newly elected Pope Julius II in Rome sent for Michelangelo. He wanted him to work on a very grand tomb. It was to be a huge centrepiece in the new St Peter's in the Vatican.
- Michelangelo began on this immediately, but the tomb of Pope Julius was to be the greatest frustration of his life for the next forty years.
- He made several starts and changes as the Pope kept changing his mind.
- There were to have been about forty large figures but the only finished figure, *The Dying Slave*, is in the Louvre in Paris.
- Four unfinished slaves are in the Accademia in Florence.

Pope Julius II and St Peter's

- Pope Julius II had a vision of restoring Renaissance Rome to the glory of ancient times.
- He began a huge amount of work on buildings. One of these was a huge new church of St Peter's but first the old Basilica that had stood there since the fourth century was demolished.
- Stone from the Coliseum was used to build St Peter's.

Moses

- There were to have been four prophets on Pope Julius's tomb but *Moses* was the only one finished. This is one Michelangelo's greatest sculptures.
- Frowning and majestic he holds the tablets of stone given to him by God in his huge veined hand.
- He glares about with an air of authority made all the more intense by the left hand intertwined in the folds of his mighty beard.
- One leg is pulled under the seated figure but the other is strong and tense. He figure looks set to leap into action at any second.

Florence Pietà

- Madonna and child groups were a constant theme of Michelangelo's art.
- He had deep religious faith and made several other pietàs.
- The *Florence Pietà* is one of his most moving works.
- Its contrasts greatly with the Rome *Pietà* created half a century earlier. This work shows a deliberately awkward pose and it is almost medieval in spirit.
- The hooded figure appears to be a self-portrait. It shows the artist to be tired, sad and utterly disillusioned with the world.

Painting

- Michelangelo was upset and angry when Pope Julius decided not to continue with the tomb and to spend the money on the new St Peter's instead.
- The Pope asked Michelangelo to paint the ceiling of the largest chapel in the Vatican, the Sistine Chapel.
- Michelangelo protested that he was a sculptor and that painting was an inferior art, but eventually he was persuaded to undertake the project.
- It turned out to be his greatest achievement.
- He painted the ceiling as an illusion of architecture decorated with sculptural-like figures.
- Michelangelo dismissed his assistants and worked on the fresco entirely alone.
- Working with tremendous dedication and energy, the great artwork took him only four years to complete.

The ceiling of the Sistine Chapel

- The ceiling is divided into three groups that tell the stories of the creation of the world, the creation and fall of man, and the story of Noah.
- All around are the prophets who foretold the coming of Christ and in the corners there are idealised nude youths.

God the Father

- Michelangelo created an entirely new imagery for his figures that have come to be accepted to this day.

- God is portrayed as a stern but athletic figure reaching upwards to the heavens.
- He creates light and then wheels around to form the planets with an easy gesture.

The Creation of Adam

- The most famous scene on the ceiling is the *Creation of Adam.*
- God creates surges across the empty sky and reaches out to the reclining figure of Adam.
- The spark of life is passed from God to man through outstretched fingers that almost touch.

The Creation of Adam, detail from the Sistine Chapel

Colours

- Traditionally it had been said that Michelangelo was more suited to sculpture because his colours were so subdued and dull.
- However when the ceiling was cleaned in the 1980s, the removal of years of grime revealed Michelangelo's work in brilliant colours. The frescoes were restored to wonderfully vivid lemons, lime greens, pinks and intense blues.

The altar wall: The Last Judgement

- Pope Julius II died within one year of the completion of the Sistine Chapel ceiling and Michelangelo spent time in Florence after that.
- He returned to Rome twenty years later to paint the largest single fresco of the century. This was a fresco of the Last Judgement on the Altar Wall of the Sistine Chapel.
- The scene itself is quite traditional but the figures are highly unusual.
- The placing of such a scene on the east rather than the traditional west was highly unusual.
- The central image of the scene is Christ in Judgement.
- He is more Greek God than a traditional image of Jesus. With a sweeping movement of the right hand he gestures the damned from his presence and calls the saved towards him.
- His mother Mary is by his side.
- On either side of Christ are the saints who have been martyred for their faith.
- Some hold instruments of their gruesome deaths. Among them St Bartholomew clutches the knife with which he was skinned alive and in the other hand holds his skin. Michelangelo has placed his own portrait on the skin.
- On the lowest level hell swirling figures are carried off in a void.

The Last Judgement, Michelangelo

'Reform' of the nude figures

- After it was completed *The Last Judgement* was greatly criticised.
- Objections to its interpretation grew and this was particularly directed against the nude figures.
- A few months before his death, Michelangelo was informed that it was to be 'reformed' according to the artistic policy of the Council of Trent. This had brought in a total banishment of the nude in religious art.
- Michelangelo's figures were made 'decent' and clothing was painted over the figures. They have remained clothed ever since

The position of the artist in society

- Michelangelo established the power and independence of the artist, which was fundamentally different from earlier periods.
- He had his own ideas and expressed his personal vision. There were two things that made this possible:
  - The position of artists was greatly uplifted because of the influence of Alberti's book;
  - An open, tolerant, art-loving atmosphere among patrons and high society had been fostered.
- The Reformation was to change this back and the Counter-Reformation re-established a rigid Church control over religious imagery in art.

Architecture

- The architect Donato Bramante began the design of the new St Peter's but the Pope asked Michelangelo to take over the project.
- By this time Michelangelo was eighty-one years old. At first he was reluctant but he later became deeply involved in the project. He disliked Bramante intensely but respected his plans.
- Michelangelo centralised the entire space with a design for a huge dome based on the Dome of Sainta Maria del Fiore in Florence.
- Michelangelo did not live to see the dome in place. Only the drum (base on which a dome rests) had been completed when he died.

The Dome of St Peter's, Michelangelo

- The dome itself was completed by another architect but Michelangelo's design is still very impressive.
- Corinthian columns in pairs on the drum give the appearance of being part of the stonework but in fact stand away from it like buttresses.
- The whole effect creates a strong vertical upward movement that culminates in the dome above.

- The nave of St Peter's was later lengthened, so in order to fully appreciate Michelangelo's dome, one has to stand well away from the building.

Raphaello Sanzio or Raphael (1483–1520)

- After Leonardo and Michelangelo, the third great name associated with the High Renaissance is Raphael. He did not create an independent or new style, but rather learned from older artists.
- Raphael was born in Urbino. He was first trained by his father, a man of culture at the court of Urbino.
- Raphael's father introduced the boy to advanced artistic ideas and humanistic philosophy. This formed the basis for the development of his extraordinary talent.

Influences

Perugino

- Raphael worked as an assistant with the artist Perugino in a large and thriving workshop and it was here that he gained extensive professional knowledge.
- Raphael absorbed Perugino's calm style and the sweet expressions on the faces of the figures in his artworks.
- These expressions became very much part of Raphael's own figures.

Michelangelo and Leonardo

- In Florence, Raphael learned from Leonardo and Michelangelo by copying their drawings.
- He absorbed their style into his own paintings and he developed their techniques, bringing Renaissance art to its most classical and serene.

Rome

- Raphael made his way to Rome, where he made a deep impression on Pope Julius II.
- He was put in sole charge of painting four large rooms in papal apartments in the Vatican.
- His personality greatly helped his success. He was not as clever as Leonardo nor had he Michelangelo's powerful drive, but he was known for being even-tempered and easy to work with. He completed commissions very quickly without fuss or disagreement.
- Unfortunately Raphael's remarkable career was very short; he died on his thirty-seventh birthday.
- He is buried in the Pantheon in Rome.

Madonnas

- Raphael is best known for his many images of the Madonna.
- These were mostly painted during his time in Florence and Leonardo's influence is very clear.

La Belle Jardinière

- This features the Madonna and child with St John the Baptist.
- Raphael has adopted Leonardo's pyramidal shape, similar to the *Virgin of the Rocks*.
- The figures are realistic in naturalistic poses but they are idealised.
- The use of sfumato has a softening effect at the edges.

The Madonna of the Goldfinch

- Michelangelo's influence can be seen in this work by Raphael.
- The baby Jesus stretches across his mother's knee.
- The young St John offers him a goldfinch, a symbol of Christ's passion.
- The mother gently helps her son accept this gift.

Madonna della Sedia (Madonna of the Chair)

- *Madonna of the Chair* is the most popular of all Raphael's Madonnas.
- Raphael chose a circular shape for this painting. A circular shape or *tondo* is difficult to work with because there is no top or bottom.
- Raphael was a master of composition and he adapts the figures to the outline.
- The figure of Virgin and the child follow the curve making them more closely entwined.
- Jesus is the centre of the picture and his elbow forms the pivotal point.
- Raphael was working in Rome when Michelangelo was painting the ceiling of the Sistine Chapel. This

The Madonna della Sedia, Raphael

may have influenced his unusual combination of strong red, blue, orange and bright green.

The Stanze (School of Athens)

- Raphael's most celebrated work is in the Vatican. This was done for Pope Julius II as part of his own residence.
- The works here are known as the Stanze Raphael.
- The most famous of these compositions is in the first of the rooms called Stanza della Segnatura.
- Important papal documents were signed there and it was also a personal library for Pope Julius II.

The School of Athens, Raphael

- The decoration celebrates the importance of books and learning.

- It features the ancient Greek philosophers Plato and Aristotle at the centre of the composition. They are placed in an imaginary architectural setting.
- These masters of science and philosophy are in fact portraits of well-known figures. Plato is thought to have Leonardo da Vinci's face. Michelangelo represents the Greek philosopher Heraclitus seated in front with head propped on one elbow.
- The groups everywhere are engaged in lively debate.
- Men of all ages listen attentively to Socrates as he emphasises points on the fingers of his left hand.

Portraits

- Raphael was also known for his very fine portraits.
- These include impressive images of the two great Renaissance Popes.

Portrait of Pope Julius II

- The portrait shows this normally aggressive and impatient man in a quiet and thoughtful pose.
- The artist has fully grasped the strength of character of his sitter, especially in the emotional intensity of the eyes.
- The hand gripping the arm of his throne also hints at a deep, restless energy.

Portrait of Pope Leo X

- *Pope Leo X* created a great sensation when it was painted.
- The Medici Pope was greatly criticised for his failure to deal with the Reformation effectively.
- He was said to have been more interested in the arts than in the Church.
- The portrait is very far from an idealised image of this plump and short-sighted man.
- It does however capture his character, while suggesting power and splendour.
- In the painting, the pope has just glanced up from examination of one of his beautifully illuminated manuscripts.
- This and the finely carved bell on the table indicate his interest in the arts.
- His richly brocaded cassock and lush velvet cape are depicted with the greatest care.
- The rich red tones make it one of Raphael's most admired works.
- It features also two cardinals, both of whom were related to Pope Leo X.

Venice

Venice prospered long after Florence and Rome to become the most splendid city in Italy. Known as the 'Queen of the Adriatic' the city was at the crossroads of east and west and its commercial fleet dominated eastern trade with Europe. This powerful independent city state was the only one to have an overseas empire and it had an exotic mix of cultures. Its unique style of building made it the spectacular city we know today.

Painting in Venice

- Colour was the more important element in Venetian painting.
- Paint was applied directly to the canvas and very loose brushwork resulted in a smooth, velvety texture and a very distinctive style.

Light and colour

- With soft light reflecting on the blue lagoons of Venice, sharp edges tend to be blurred and everything is bathed in a soft radiant light. This may have influenced the painters.
- Light played an important role. It helped them create atmosphere and mystery, particularly in landscape painting.

Painting on canvas

- One of the major contributions made by Venice to painting was the development of oil painting on canvas.
- The damp atmosphere made fresco painting on plastered walls impossible, so artists stretched canvas over wooden frames and primed it with white gesso.
- This allowed the light to glow through layers of oily paint and glazes.

Artists in Venice

Giorgione da Castlefranco (1478–1510)

- Little is known of Giorgione (meaning 'big Giorgio').
- His dreamlike and mysterious painting brought the new word *poesie* (meaning 'visual poetry') to Renaissance art.
- He died young and his pupil Titian probably finished several of his paintings. Only a few can be definitely attributed to him.
- All of his paintings have a strange, mysterious quality filled with a hazy light that adds to the moody, romantic atmosphere.

The Tempest

- A fascinating painting known as *The Tempest* is one of Giorgione's few surviving works.
- The mood stems from the vibrant brightness of a single flash of lightning just before a storm, which makes for sharp contrasts of light and shadow.
- A man stands near the ruins of the architecture and a mother in the foreground cradles her child under the trees.
- However the exact meaning of this atmospheric landscape and its figures remains a mystery.

The Tempest, Giorgione

The Sleeping Venus

- Giorgione's *The Sleeping Venus* is one of the most perfect Renaissance paintings.
- The goddess of love sleeps in the peace of the countryside, unaware of her nakedness.
- The painting is bathed in soft sunlight, creating an atmosphere of the poetic beauty.

The Sleeping Venus, Giorgione

- Giorgione's painting aspired towards a very particular type of pastoral poetry called *L'Arcadia*. This was an imaginary untroubled paradise where everyone could live in perfect peace and harmony

Titian (1485–1576)

- Tiziano Vecellio or Titian became Painter to the Republic of Venice. He was the most expressive painter of his time and has remained one of the great names in European art.
- He learned his technical skills from Giorgione and his rich colours and painterly technique are greatly admired.
- Titian left a huge body of work on almost every subject. When he died at about ninety years of age, he was a rich man and the most famous artist in Europe.

Paintings by Titian

Venus of Urbino

- Titian adapted Giorgione's ideas in a number of works, the best-known of which is *Venus of Urbino*.
- The similarities are immediately obvious but Giorgione's silent and untouched landscape is now a private room.
- The pose is almost the same but considerably more erotic.

Venus of Urbino, Titian

- Titian's girl is awake, quite aware of her audience and conscious of her charms.
- The picture was painted to celebrate a marriage and it has many symbolic references:
  - The little dog curled up on the bed symbolises faithfulness.
  - The maids in the background are opening a 'marriage' chest.

Concert Champêtre

- Titian worked as Giorgione's assistant until Giorgione's death in 1510 and some works once attributed to Giorgione are now considered to have been by Titian.
- *Concert Champêtre* (Pastoral Concert) is another mysterious painting.
- This was considered the finest of Giorgione's works, but it is now believed that Titian painted, or at least finished, this.

The Assumption

- The altarpiece of the *Assumption of the Virgin* in the church of Santa Maria Gloriosa dei Frari in Venice broke with tradition.
- Bold colour and innovative composition are on display here.
- The novel portrayal of the Virgin clothed in vibrant red and twisting dramatically created some controversy at the time.

Bacchus and Ariadne

- Titian was also commissioned to paint a number of mythological compositions.
- One of these was the dramatic moment from classical poetry when the wine god Bacchus falls in love with Princess Ariadne, daughter of the King of Crete.
- The real theme of *Bacchus and Ariadne* is the idea of love at first sight.
- The picture is famous for its spectacular colours.
- Intense blue ultramarine and red vermilion make for stunning contrasts with the blue of the sky.

Bacchus and Ariadne, Titian

- The artist chose a beautiful gold–orange pigment for Bacchus' sash.

Ecce Homo

- One of Titian's deeply spiritual paintings was painted when the artist was almost eighty years old.
- He painted the subject many times but *Ecce Homo* in the National Gallery of Ireland is perhaps the finest example.
- The bright yellow glow of the halo shows this 'man of sorrow' with his face in shadow and downcast eyes.
- Soft painterly tones make this a deeply moving image of a gentle Christ bound, tortured, beaten and crowned with thorns.

Ecce Homo, Titian

2006 Ordinary Level paper: Section II, Question 9

Name **one** work by either Michelangelo (1475–1564) **or** Raphael (1483–1520) and describe and discuss it under the following headings:

- subject matter
- composition/design
- medium used
- style

and

Give a short general account of the work of either Michelangelo **or** Raphael.

2008 Ordinary Level paper: Section I, Question 9

Primavera by Sandro Botticelli (1445–1510) is illustrated below.

Answer (a) and (b).

(a) Describe and discuss this work under the following headings:

- subject matter
- composition
- colour

(b) Name and give a short description of one other work by Botticelli.

Use sketches to illustrate your answer.

2007 Higher Level paper: Section I, Question 10

Describe and discuss the work of Donatello (1386–1466), referring to at least two named works by him

and

Outline the main innovations he brought to sculpture during the early Renaissance.

Illustrate your answer.

2008 Higher Level paper: Section I, Question 9

The art of perspective was developed during the Early Renaissance in Florence.

Discuss this statement making detailed reference to a named work of art by Paolo Uccello (1397–1475)

and

Discuss briefly another work by Uccello **or** a work by any artist of the early Renaissance that clearly shows the use of perspective.

Illustrate your answer.

2009 Higher Level paper: Section I, Question 10

Describe and discuss the life and work of Sandro Botticelli (1445–1510), referring to two named allegorical paintings by him

and

Describe in detail the symbolism in one of his works.

Use sketches to illustrate your answer.

2009 Higher Level paper: Section I, Question 11

Name, describe and discuss the sculpture shown below, making reference to the artist, subject matter, composition, depiction of space and treatment of the human figure

and

Name and briefly discuss one other work by this artist.

Use sketches to illustrate your answer.

SAMPLE EXAM QUESTION

The depiction of three-dimensional space through knowledge of perspective played a major part in the work of the Early Renaissance painters.

With this statement in mind discuss *The Tribute Money* by Masaccio (1401–28), shown below, and write a brief note on Masaccio and on one other work by him.

Illustrate your answer.

TIPS

- When you are given a colour illustration it is very important to look carefully at the work. Refer to it constantly, making it the key element of your essay.
- Note that this question relates to 'the depiction of three-dimensional space and perspective', so make sure your points are relevant to the discussion.
- The choice of another work is quite open and another fresco from the Brancacci Chapel such as the *Expulsion of Adam and Eve* would also be acceptable.
- Remember that this question does **not** ask you to simply write an account of Masaccio's life and works, so choose your essay points with care!

SAMPLE ANSWER

The Tribute Money is a fresco by the Renaissance artist Masaccio. It is a huge painting and it shows the full range of his talents. Its depiction of space in particular shows his enthusiasm for mathematics and geometry, as well as a range of influences from his contemporaries. The painting has been restored a number of times over the years because it was damaged in a fire in 1771, which darkened the colours. However, when the layers of smut were cleaned away the powerful image that we see today was uncovered in all its vibrant colour and detail.

Masaccio

Tomaso Cassai, nicknamed Masaccio, worked in an era where change was embraced and innovative thinking was breathing new life into art. This time of intense artistic activity was later called the 'Renaissance', a French word meaning rebirth. It began in Florence in the early fifteenth century and was inspired by the literature, language, culture and art of classical Rome and Greece.

Early Renaissance artists in Florence are sometimes referred to as the first generation and Masaccio was a pivotal figure within this group. He was influenced by the artist Giotto who had broken the tradition of Byzantine painting one hundred years earlier. Masaccio used the same techniques to depict solid, lifelike figures in a realistic three-dimensional space. Like Giotto, he used expressions and gestures to convey a narrative, but he was also influenced by contemporary artists Donatello and Brunelleschi.

Donatello had recently produced some very realistic and lifelike sculpture and Masaccio's blocky, sculptural figures show the influence of these graceful works. Leaving aside the ornate splendour of previous compositions, Masaccio favoured this newer, simpler style and he developed a new humanity in his figures.

Brunelleschi's perspective studies

Early in the fifteenth century Filippo Brunelleschi had devised a mathematical means to represent space with dramatic reality when he carried out a series of optical experiments. His theory was simple: that the size of an object appears to get smaller the farther away it is from the eye. Brunelleschi worked on his experiments using mirrors and careful calculations and founded a mathematical system based on a central vanishing point. This meant that all lines leading into the distance came together with the horizon line at a single point in the picture. He passed on this system of linear perspective to his friends in Florence and soon artists like Masaccio began to use the method to create realistic spaces in their paintings.

The wealthy Brancacci family gave Masaccio the opportunity to work on a huge scale and use these innovative methods in his monumental work of powerful realism. The affluent bankers had been patrons of a little chapel in the Church of Santa Maria del Carmine in Florence for generations and they commissioned Masaccio to paint a magnificent fresco series based on the life of St Peter. The three walls of the chapel are painted with scenes from the gospels.

The Tribute Money is the most dominant scene and it occupies the upper half of one wall on the left hand side. It relates to an unimportant event from the gospel of St Matthew about a tax to enter the city of Capernaum, but there is an interesting reason for the choice of such a scene. The Brancacci family were bankers and therefore the scene had particular relevance for them because in it Jesus is shown to have respect for the town's taxes and this sent out a message to all of Florence that banking and tax collecting was a necessary part of life. References to politics in Florence often featured in the artwork of the day.

A three-part composition

The composition is in three parts, following the traditional manner of featuring several episodes of a story in one painting. The central part shows the tax collector asking Peter for money. Peter refuses but Jesus points to the lake suggesting that it is right to pay what is due. The left part of the painting shows Peter taking money from a fish's mouth at the lakeside and the third scene Peter gives the coin to the tax collector at the gate.

Masaccio's strong and monumental figures accentuate the smooth roundness of the flesh and the light on the clothing creates a sculptural-like shadow, adding greatly to the dramatic impact of the story.

Peter and Christ both echo each other's pose, standing with one knee bent and one arm outstretched. Both images of the tax collector mirror also each other. The effect of this is to lock the main characters together as a single unit within the composition.

Perspective

Elements of the new art of perspective are clearly seen in this work. Under a beautiful blue sky with white clouds, the picture shows snow-capped mountains fading into the distance with trees and farmhouses featuring in the middle distance; all are in perfect perspective.

Also Peter and the tax collector are framed by the crisp architectural outlines of the building on the far right, with the doorway and steps defining the space where the men stand. Even though all the heads of the figures are more or less on one line, their feet tell us how far or near they are in the painting. Jesus is clearly set apart from the group in his pale-coloured robe. If, however, one follows the perspective lines of the roof and steps of the porch they all meet at Jesus' face.

The Trinity

In even more dramatic use of perspective Massacio painted another famous fresco on the wall of St Maria Novella in Florence. *The Trinity* was one of the first paintings where all the lines of perspective converge to a single vanishing point at eye level. It gives the illusion of a small chapel on the wall in which the three persons of the Trinity are present. God the Father dominates the scene. He is above the eye level of the viewer, holding the arms of the cross on which Jesus hangs. Mary and John are at eye level at the base and on either side kneel the patrons. Below the viewer's line of vision there is a painting of a stone coffin that tilts outwards to show a skeleton inside it. Just above it, written in Latin, are the words of an ancient warning that says: 'I was what you are and what I am you shall be.' Before painting this fresco Masaccio drew out the lines of perspective using string stretched between nails. The marks of the string pressing into the plaster can still be seen as can the holes for the nails. The painting has suffered a lot of damage over the years but it has been well restored.

Influences

Masaccio died at the age of twenty-seven, before the frescoes at the Brancacci Chapel were completed; yet his figures remain as a tribute to him. Other legendry characters would come to view them in the years after his death, the most important being Michelangelo. Who knows the impact that Masaccio's masterpieces had on the young man who went on to create the great Sistine Chapel in Rome. Masaccio's genius most certainly inspired many other Renaissance artists and his works still have a profound impact on the viewer. Most certainly it sent shivers down my spine when I saw them for the first time in Florence not so long ago.

exam focus

Always examine the question that gives choice of a work in a category. It may well give you the opportunity to write about something special such as in the following extract relating to Question 11 from the 2005 Higher Level paper.

SAMPLE EXAM QUESTION

Discuss one of the following works in detail, making reference to style, composition/design, technique, and the period in which it was produced:

- *The Last Judgement* by Michelangelo (1475 –1564)
- *St Jerome in his Study* by Dürer (1471–1528)
- *The Night Watch* by Rembrandt (1606–69)
- *The Ecstasy of St Teresa* by Bernini (1598–1680)

and

Name, describe and discuss one other work by the artist you have chosen.

Illustrate your answer.

SAMPLE ANSWER OF PART 1

Just imagine my delight last year when I was given the chance to visit the Sistine Chapel in Rome with my mother. This opportunity to view some of the biggest and most famous masterpieces in the world came last Easter and for me undoubtedly the most impressive of all was *The Last Judgement* on the Altar Wall of the chapel.

This late masterpiece by Michelangelo was commissioned by Pope Paul III Farnese twenty years after the completion of ceiling in the Sistine Chapel in 1534. Before any work could be carried out two earlier frescoes and two windows above the altar had to be removed and a new wall was built with an inward slant to prevent dust settling on it. Then in 1541 Michelangelo completed *The Last Judgement* after working unaccompanied on it for seven years.

The painting has all the imagery of the end of the world. The dead souls are rising up to face God and their unknown future...heaven or hell. This subject was rarely used on an altar but the Pope chose to have the graphic imagery here as a warning to Catholics to adhere to their faith during the turmoil of the Reformation. *The Last Judgement* is also a disturbing reminder of Michelangelo's own tormented attitude towards his faith.

The figures in this composition had the most dramatic impact on me. Ripped from their graves, the souls of the dead rise to face Christ who, with his mother Mary at his side, is the focal point of the painting. No one is sure if his gesture is welcoming or the opposite but I am quite clear that he is showing no sympathy at all for the damned souls and is hurling them down to the demons in hell, where they are shoved from Charon's Boat into the depths of Hades.

The figure of Minos in hell is taken from Dante's *Inferno*. An interesting point about Minos is that he has the ears of an ass; it is actually a portrait of courtier Biagio da Cesena who openly criticised Michelangelo's use of nude figures in the fresco. All the figures including Christ were nude originally, but sometime after the completion of *The Last Judgement* the Pope ordered that they be covered by clothes. The fresco was actually repainted by one of Michelangelo's students who subsequently became known as the Britches Maker. Michelangelo has also included a self-portrait in the work. The martyr St Bartholomew who was put to death by being skinned alive holds up a knife with one hand and his skin with the other for all to see. Michelangelo chose to paint his own image on the skin and to me this says a lot about his tortured mentality at the time.

Eimear Ní Mhúrchú, 2010

TIP

- For part two of the question, it would be useful for this student to choose another work she saw on her trip to Rome. This could be a scene from the ceiling of the Sistine Chapel, the sculpture of the *Piéta* in the Vatican, or the statue of Moses on the tomb of Michelangelo. She could even discuss Michelangelo's Dome on St Peter's. Continuing her essay in this direct, story-like style would be advisable.

Impressionism and Twentieth-Century Art Movements

Art, politics and revolution

Impressionism is one of the most popular of all art movements in Europe. The paintings are colourful, cheerful in mood and easy to understand, but the artists who produced these works were considered dangerous revolutionaries in their own time. The paintings were considered ridiculous and were mocked and jeered after their first exhibition. Art education in France was very rigid and artists had to follow a very traditional route to become successful. The small group of artists who broke with this system in the mid-nineteenth century became known as the Impressionists. It was many years before their work was accepted and their groundbreaking innovations in painting fully recognised and admired.

Forerunners of Impressionism

The Academy

- The government of France controlled the *Académie des Beaux-Arts*.
- Students entered the studio of an established artist and studied according to the Academic system.
- The Academy exhibited the work of artists once a year. This exhibition was called the Salon.
- The system did not suit all artists and in the mid-nineteenth century some searched for other ways to express ideas.

Realism

- Gustave Courbet set out to shock society out of its state of complacency with a new art movement called Realism.
- Realists favoured ordinary scenes of modern life over historical, mythological and religious subjects. They wanted 'truth, not prettiness'.
- *Burial at Ornans*, a painting by Courbet, was exhibited at the 1850–51 Salon. It created an 'explosive reaction' and brought Courbet instant fame.

Barbizon painters

- Artists from the Realist movement worked out of doors (*en plein air*).
- They chose to live outside of Paris in the village of Barbizon, where they sketched directly from nature on the edge of the Forest of Fontainebleau.
- Peasants, houses, the forest and the fields were their sources of inspiration.

- Camille Corot painted out of doors in Normandy, Brittany and around the Forest of Fontainebleau.
- Corot was a transitional figure in painting and was highly influential on younger painters.
- He praised nature and urged his followers to hold fast to the first impression they received from a scene.
- In the end he criticised the Impressionists and condemned their work, but Claude Monet and Pierre Auguste Renoir learned a great deal from him.

Édouard Manet

- The city of Paris was redeveloped during the 1860s.
- In his paintings, Édouard Manet included fashionably-dressed people as an image of a prosperous modern city.
- The public regarded Manet with great suspicion.

Towards Impressionism

- Wealthy industrialists and the new middle class were the art-buying public in the mid-nineteenth century.
- They trusted the 'experts' of the Academy, so their taste in art was rather conservative. Their preference was for story pictures with historical or moral content.
- One of the most popular subjects was classical myths and legends of ancient Greece and Rome.
- Artworks on these subjects were considered serious and respectable. Nude figures were acceptable in this context, but very strict rules applied to the depiction of nude women in artworks generally.
- Female subjects could not look obviously sensual, but were considered perfectly acceptable as nymphs or figures from ancient history.

Jean Auguste Dominique Ingres

- Ingres is associated with Academic art at its most sterile.
- He was a very successful painter and his technique was academically perfect.
- He believed that paint should be smooth 'as the skin of an onion'.
- To achieve his vision of ideal beauty he often distorted the proportions of his figures.
- He became director of the French Academy and held the position for over forty years. His ideals developed into a rigid set of formulae.
- Artists who followed his formula were guaranteed success and respectability; those who did not were destined for mediocrity.

The Valpinçon Bather

- This one of the finest works by Ingres. It was criticised originally because of its deliberately distorted proportions in the model's right leg.
- The back view was also considered highly unusual.
- However, the painting cleverly draws the spectator into the tranquil setting, with subtle light.
- The hidden face adds mystery to the scene.

La Source

- This painting by Ingres shows a young woman standing at the edge of a rock pool.
- She stretches her arms slowly to empty a water jar over her shoulder. One leg is seductively placed forward in classical pose and she gazes at the viewer with lips apart.
- Despite the seductive pose, the young woman displays a pure, virginal quality.

Influence on artists

- Ingres' work was highly influential on other artists and the style became very popular.
- *The Birth of Venus* by Alexandre Cabanel was the hit of the 1863 Salon exhibition.
- It was everything that visitors to the Salon sought. The figure is quietly erotic but idealised, passive and without character.
- She is an image of perfection, with masses of luxuriant hair.

The Valpinçon Bather, Jean Dominique Ingres, Louvre

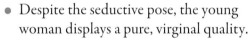

Visit www.metmuseum.org for essays on many artists, including Impressionists and Post-Impressionists.

The Birth of Venus, Alexandre Cabanel

Modernity: Édouard Manet

Édouard Manet was a student of art in the 1850s, when Gustave Courbet's work was causing controversy. He was deeply influenced by the Realist energy but the provincial paintings were not to the young Manet's taste.

A modern revolution

- Manet wanted to work in truly modern style.
- He greatly admired paintings by the old masters and had a clear vision of how to modernise these grand traditions in a specifically French context.
- Unfortunately this vision did not fit with the Academic manner.

A well-to-do background

- Manet was born into a prosperous upper middle class family.
- After his father's death in 1862 he inherited a considerable fortune that made him independently wealthy.
- He trained in the standard Academic system but it frustrated him. He hated the artificial studio light and affected poses of the models.

key point

Manet said: 'I paint what I see and not what others choose to see.'

A new direction in art

- Manet's art took a new direction when he rejected some of the Academic values.
- Instead of a light source from one side, he chose a direct source like sunlight that made strong colour contrasts and exaggerated light and darkness.
- He left out the in-between grey tones and this tended to 'flatten out' his shadows.
- This element of his work was greatly criticised, even ridiculed by the critics, when he exhibited.
- Manet's earlier paintings were worked with thick paint and dark backgrounds. This style was drawn from seventeenth-century Spanish artists like Velázquez.

Absinthe Drinker

- This was Manet's first submission to the Salon of 1859.
- It had a definite Spanish influence.
- The subject of a down-and-out alcoholic in Paris was unacceptable to society and the jury rejected the painting.

Manet and the Paris Salon

- Manet never set out to be a rebel. He had the highest regard for the Paris Salon and wanted more than anything to make his name there.
- This never changed throughout his life. Even when he suffered rejection and ridicule from the Salon, he respected the institution.
- In 1861 his painting *Spanish Singer* was commended, but this success was short-lived.
- For the next twenty years the Salon became Manet's battleground; all his major submissions were completely rejected and this upset him greatly.

Salon des Refusés

- In 1863 the Salon jury rejected an unusually large number of paintings.
- The Emperor Napoleon III intervened and declared that a separate exhibition of rejected work should be held, giving the public a chance to view the artworks and make up their own minds. This resulted in the Salon des Refusés (Salon for the refused).

- Spurred on by the media, people turned up at the Salon des Refusés to mock the work that the 'experts' had rejected.
- Manet's submissions at the Salon des Refusés caused particular outrage.

Le Déjeuner sur l'Herbe

- This is Manet's adaption of a well-known Renaissance painting by Titian, *Concert Champêtre*.
- In Manet's modern interpretation, men in everyday modern dress are placed alongside a nude female.
- The artwork caused a great scandal and became one of the most talked-about works at the exhibition.

Le Dejeuner sur l'Herbe Manet

A Modern Olympia

- This is another of Manet's adaptations of a Renaissance painting. Here he uses a different work by Titian: *Venus of Urbino*.
- Manet named his work *Olympia* but did not submit it to the Salon.
- His friends persuaded him to put it forward for the next Salon in 1865.
- The jury accepted the painting but Manet's fears were confirmed.
- The reaction from the public was one of real hatred. No one appreciated his fine painting methods, splendid colour harmonies and subtle simplification of light and shade.
- The critics savaged the artwork and the jury ordered that it be moved to the top corner of the wall.

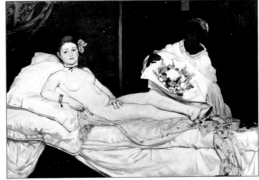

A Modern Olympia, Manet

- The woman in *Olympia* is nude. She is quite unlike the demure classical figure depicted in Titian's painting.
- This is a modern young woman with a neck-ribbon and bracelet.
- She gazes at the viewer with a cool, confident stare.
- The flat, dark background contrasts with the light skin tones.
- A black cat appears in place of the quietly sleeping dog in Titian's painting; this particularly irritated the critics.
- One critic said: 'The model is puny, the bed covered with cat's footprints, the general effect ugly, but that could be forgiven if it were truthful; even the least beautiful woman has bones, muscles, skin and some sort of colour, whereas on this woman the flesh colour is dirty and the modelling non-existent.'

Manet's character

- Manet was shattered by the harsh criticisms of his work.
- Because of the reaction to *Olympia*, he never again tried this kind of imagery and yet his work continued to cause controversy.
- Because of the controversy surrounding Manet's work, people tended to think that he was a rough, revolutionary type.
- This was very far from the truth and he was known for his elegance and charm.
- He had a cutting wit but his friends all spoke of his goodness and generosity of spirit.
- Even the critics stressed his 'agreeable character and correct appearance'.

Music in the Tuileries Gardens

- This painting depicts a gathering of sophisticated people in the gardens of the Tuileries Palace.
- These gardens were an attractive place for the fashionable people of Paris to meet and to be seen.
- The painting features many portraits of the artist's friends, as well as a self-portrait.
- The influence of the new art of photography is seen in the way some figures are cut in half by the framing edge of the canvas.
- Manet sold the painting in 1870.

Association with the Impressionists

- Manet mixed in the artistic circles that gathered in the cafés of Paris.
- Younger painters regarding him as the leader of the revolt against the traditions of French art.
- Claude Monet and other members of the Impressionist group tried to get him to join them.
- Manet admired and encouraged the Impressionists but consistently refused to exhibit with them.
- He was, however, influenced by the group's innovations in painting.
- They encouraged Manet to use colour instead of grey or black, particularly in shadow, and to observe the effect of light on water.
- Manet was happy to play the part of modern master to younger artists but continued to suffer from rejection at the Salon.
- His name was now linked with the Impressionists and he received the same hostile reviews that they suffered.

The Bar at the Folies-Bergère

- This is one of the best-known of Manet's paintings.
- The *Folies-Bergère* attracted a wide audience, particularly men on the look-out for casual relationships.
- Manet persuaded one of the barmaids to pose in his studio.

- Every detail in the painting has been rendered with meticulous realism. A huge mirror in the background reflects the crowd of people gathered together talking and drinking.
- This painting brought Manet the recognition he had sought. He received a medal of honour and this meant automatic acceptance in the Salon.
- Acceptance came late for Manet. By the time he was given a medal of honour, he was very ill.
- He had to finish the painting by sitting with his leg up. This leg was amputated the following spring, but he never recovered and he died in April 1883 aged fifty-one.
- After his death, his work was exhibited at the École des Beaux Arts.
- Five years later at the International Exhibition held in Paris his works were greatly admired.

Impressionism

The Impressionists

- Some of the artists who met Édouard Manet regularly to discuss art became better known as the Impressionists.
- These artists had developed a particular style of painting by working directly from nature out of doors.
- They had tried on several occasions to have their work accepted by the Salon.
- This never came to pass, so in April 1874 they held an independent exhibition.
- The artists included <u>Edgar Degas</u>, <u>Claude Monet</u>, Paul Cézanne, <u>Pierre Auguste Renoir</u>, Camille Pissarro, Alfred Sisley and Berthe Morisot.
- The paintings were mostly simple scenes of landscapes, cityscapes and everyday life.
- They were painted quickly with loose brushstrokes. The artists felt that this captured the life and play of light on the subject better.
- This broke almost every rule of the Academy and visitors to the exhibition were shocked. They could not understand the work and thought it unfinished.
- Critics said that the Impressionists couldn't draw and that their colours were vulgar.

The term 'Impressionism'

- The famous name came about because of a painting in this first exhibition by Claude Monet. It was entitled *Impression Sunrise*.
- One of the critics made fun of this by calling it an impression of nature and wondering 'who were these "Impressionists"?'
- The group kept the name and had seven more exhibitions.
- They struggled for the next twelve years to gain acceptance. Gradually their popularity grew and they began to have success with the buyers.
- In time Impressionism became one of the most influential modern movements in art.

Impression Sunrise

Impression Sunrise, Monet

- This painting by Monet showed sunrise over the sea at Le Havre.
- His aim was to create an impression of the rapidly changing, shimmering orange light of the morning sun on the water.
- He wanted to capture the intense brightness with contrasting complementary colours, thereby making the primary colours brighter.

Innovations of Impressionist painting

Impressionist artists:

- Painted directly from nature, out of doors.
- Avoided black and mixed complementary colours to achieve dark tones.
- Examined the effects of bright sunshine or light on water and snow.
- Noticed blue and purple shadows in snow.
- Observed changes in colour on objects in different light.
- Used unmixed primary colours and small strokes to capture the effect of reflected light.
- Used loose brushstrokes to capture movement or quivering light.
- Placed small strokes of colour side by side on the canvas, allowing the colour to blend in the viewer's own vision.
- Went against the tradition of building up the surface in thin layers or transparent glazes.
- Placed wet paint onto wet paint to create a soft-edged effect.
- Were influenced by photography in the late nineteenth century.
- Were inspired by Japanese prints that had just become available in Paris.

key point

Quick outdoor sketching with loose brushstrokes had always been part of the Academic training. Oil sketches called *esquisses* were very similar to Impressionist paintings but finished paintings were done in the studio and had very smooth surfaces.

exam focus

Note your dates!
If the question does not mention the word 'Impressionist' it could be misleading. Question 14 on the 2005 paper asked you to discuss artistic developments in the 'second half of the nineteenth century'. In this case your answer should focus on Impressionism. A different question could expect you to discuss developments earlier than this.

key point

The development of the railway and of portable tin tubes for oil paints made it easier for the nineteenth-century Impressionists to work *en plein air*. Trains allowed them to travel to popular recreation spots and Jean Renoir, son of Pierre Auguste, wrote of his father: 'easily transportable paints in tubes led us to paint directly from nature'.

Modern subjects

- Impressionist paintings were modern, not just in style, but also in subject matter.
- The Impressionists were influenced by Édouard Manet. Unlike the Barbizon group, who painted rural scenes and peasants, the Impressionists painted modern life in Paris.
- Their paintings featured the suburbs, with fashionably-dressed people involved in leisure and entertainment activities.

Claude Monet (1840–1926)

- Claude Monet is the most famous Impressionist artist.
- He was completely dedicated to the idea of painting out of doors.
- His goal was to capture a single moment of time and light in his painting.
- He worked tirelessly to achieve this effect. Towards the end of his life his paintings became almost abstract, with swirling colours dissolving into light.

Early influences

- Monet came from Le Havre in Normandy and he began painting there.
- He then went to Paris, where he met Camille Pissarro and became interested in landscape painting.
- He met the Barbizon painters and learned to appreciate the benefits of working *en plein air*.

Paris

- He enrolled at Charles Gleyre's studio in Paris and met fellow students Frederic Bazille, Alfred Sisley and Pierre Auguste Renoir.
- The students regularly met after class in the Café Guerbois and had lively discussions on art with other young artists like Paul Cézanne and Edgar Degas.
- In 1865 the Salon accepted two of Monet's seascapes but the critics confused his name with Edouard Manet.

Financial difficulties

- Life became difficult for Claude Monet in the late 1860s. He had very little success at the Salon.
- Financially he was very badly off and his girlfriend Camille became pregnant.
- His large painting *Women in the Garden* was rejected by the Salon, so he abandoned figure painting.
- He spent the summer of 1869 painting riverside pictures with his friend Renoir.
- These paintings marked the real beginning of Impressionism.

La Grenouillère

- Monet and Renoir painted at La Grenouillère (the Frog Pond) on the banks of the Seine just outside Paris.
- Monet made a floating studio and sat out on the water to paint.
- Here he painted *Bathers at La Grenouillère*. The painting's long brushstrokes and dabs of colour suggest the boats and jetties and emphasise the patterns of light on water.

Japonisme

- Monet was probably influenced even at this early stage by Japanese woodblock prints.
- These were widely available at an affordable price.
- Their flat planes of bright colour offered an alternative approach to traditional landscape painting.

London

- During the Franco-Prussian War (1870–1) he took refuge in England with Pissarro.
- Monet painted the Houses of Parliament and the effect of the London fog.
- He met the dealer Durand Ruel, who was to become one of the great champions of the Impressionists.
- After his return to France, Monet lived at Argenteuil, a village on the Seine near Paris. It was here that he painted some of the most famous Impressionist artworks.
- His friends Renoir, Manet and Sisley visited him here and worked with him.
- In 1874 Monet and his colleagues decided to appeal directly to the public by organising their own exhibition.
- The exhibition created a scandal and his financial situation remained very poor but Monet persisted with his style.
- One of Monet's best-known works from this period is *Red Poppies at Argenteuil*. This picture shows his wife and son walking through a field of poppies. It was shown at the first Impressionist exhibition.

Regatta at Argenteuil

- This Monet painting is a splendid study of reflections.
- Slabs of pure colour suggest the shimmering effect of the reflections of sails and the buildings on the water.

Regatta at Argenteuil, Monet

Success

- Monet began at last to have success as an artist, but after his second son was born in 1878 his wife Camille remained seriously ill. She died a year later.
- Monet and Camille had been living with the Hochedé family, who were good friends to them.
- Alice Hochedé had cared for Camille during her illness and she and Monet remained together after her death.
- After the death of Alice's husband, she and Monet married.

Giverny

- Monet bought a house in the village of Giverny on a small river near the Seine.
- Monet lived here with Alice, Monet's two sons and the six Hochedé children.
- At Giverny he developed his famous water garden with a Japanese bridge.
- He lived here for forty-three years, painting until the end of his life. He died in 1926 at the age of eighty-six.

Water Lily Pond–Harmony in Green

- Although Monet loved plants and flowers, he was not interested in distinguishing them in a painting. He was more interested in the reflections on the water.
- In *Water Lily Pond–Harmony in Green*, the surface of the painting is a rich carpet of colour, with brushstrokes of yellow, pink and lavender woven in with the shimmering green of the plants.

Water Lily Pond – Harmony in Green, Monet

Travelling in France

- During the 1870s and 1880s Monet gradually refined his technique.
- He made many trips to scenic areas of France to study the most brilliant effects of light and colour possible.

Haystacks, End of Summer, Monet

Rouen Cathedral, Full Sunlight, Harmony in Blue and Gold, Monet

- From 1890 he concentrated on a series of pictures in which he painted the same subject at different times of the day in different lights.
- *Haystacks* and *Rouen Cathedral* are the best known examples of these.
- In 1914 he had a special studio built in the grounds of his house and here he worked on huge canvases.
- In the last years of his life, he painted a series of water lilies called *Les Grandes Decorations*. He donated these to the French state and they are now displayed as he intended in two oval-shaped rooms in the Musée d'Orangerie in Paris, bathed in natural light from the glass roof.

Camille Pissarro (1830–1903)

- Camille Pissarro was a very important figure in the Impressionist movement.
- He was about ten years older than the others and he constantly advised and encouraged them.
- He organised the exhibitions and was the one who exhibited at all eight Impressionist shows.
- As well as teaching the younger artists, he also learned from them; and yet he remained insecure about his own his work.

Working with the Impressionists

- Pissarro worked consistently in the outdoors at landscape paintings.
- He also kept a studio in Paris where he met regularly with Monet, Renoir, Sisley, Bazille and Cézanne in the Café Guerbois to discuss art.
- Pissarro often worked with Claude Monet and the two painted many winter scenes together, such as *Road to Versailles*.
- Pissarro also moved to London during the Franco-Prussian war. Here he made contact with the art dealer Durand Ruel.
- During the 1870s Pissarro combined his own work with the organisation of the Impressionist exhibitions.
- In the first exhibition in 1874 the critics condemned his landscapes as much as the others.
- He suffered considerable financial loss.

Search for perfection

- Pissarro's landscapes included river banks or views of winding roadways.
- Throughout his career he relentlessly searched for the perfect method of expressing himself.
- One of his favourite subjects was that of houses half-hidden by trees, which created a broken design over the canvas.

The Red Roofs

- This is a painting of bare winter trees, through which can be seen a cluster of houses with red roofs glistening in the winter sunshine.
- The effect of the trees against the roofs is more impressive because the rich surface is painted with small, thick brushstrokes.

The Red Roofs, Pissarro

Success at last

- Pissarro remained in difficult financial circumstances for much of his career.
- In 1892 fifty of his works sold at a major retrospective exhibition.
- At last, he could provide financial security for his wife and seven children.
- He bought the house at Eragny and painted some of his finest works in the countryside near his home.
- *Landscape at Eragny* is more freely painted compared to Pissarro's earlier work. It is a beautiful study of warm, diffused sunlight.
- Pissarro died in 1903 at the age of seventy-three.

Pierre Auguste Renoir (1841–1919)

- Pierre Auguste Renoir met Pissarro and Claude Monet at the studio in Paris where they were students.
- Monet persuaded him of the benefits of painting out of doors.
- Renoir and Monet's paintings were remarkably similar when both artists worked together in the early years.
- For a time, Renoir shared his friend's fascination for the effects of light on water, but later he focused more on the human figure.
- Some of Renoir's most enduring images are of people enjoying themselves. Smiling faces and pretty children make his paintings very appealing.
- He was often criticised for this and in defence he said: 'Why shouldn't art be pretty? There are enough unpleasant things in the world.'
- Like the other Impressionists, he endured much hardship early in his career but he eventually achieved success.
- The art dealer Durand Ruel found regular buyers for Renoir's work.
- Renoir made many studies of models and friends.
- His favourite were models from Montmartre, dressed in the latest Parisian style.

Bal at the Moulin de la Galette

- *Bal at the Moulin de la Galette* was described as the most beautiful picture of the nineteenth-century.
- In it Renoir managed to gather numerous figures together in one composition.

- He has cleverly captured facial expressions and movement.
- The sunlight filtering through the trees casts shadows on the dancing figures and creates a dappled pattern on the ground.

The Bal at the Moulin de la Galette, Renoir

Luncheon of the Boating Party

- The scene is set in a restaurant at a favourite spot for boating enthusiasts and their girlfriends.
- The woman on the left hand side with the dog is Aline Charigot, Renoir's future wife and favourite model.

Departure from Impressionism

- In the 1880s, Renoir abandoned Impressionism and no longer exhibited with his former colleagues.
- Seeking new inspiration he travelled to Italy with Aline, where he rediscovered the works of the old masters.

Luncheon of the Boating Party, Renoir

The Umbrellas

- Changes in Renoir's painting style can clearly be seen in this painting.
- The figures on the right are painted in the Impressionist style, with bright colours and loose brushwork.
- The two figures on the left are more 'finished' and subdued in colour.

The nude figure

- In later years, Renoir returned to a softer style of painting.
- He painted many scenes of bathers in the sunlight.
- These nude female figures have that soft, pearly skin texture for which Renoir has become so well known.

The Umbrellas, Renoir

A World-renowned artist

- Renoir spent his last years in the south of France. He suffered from severe arthritis but continued to paint.
- When the Louvre acquired his painting in 1919 he travelled to Paris.
- He was honoured as a world-renowned artist and was escorted through the Galleries in a wheelchair. He died shortly after his return to the south.

Alfred Sisley (1839–1899)

- Another member of the group of students from the Paris studio was Alfred Sisley.
- As an artist he tends to be overlooked in the history of Impressionism, yet he had a quiet, steady talent.
- His work is quite dramatic and powerful and his snowscapes in particular have a gentle, almost poetic quality.
- His style did not greatly appeal to the public but he worked in all the places associated with Impressionism: Bougival, Argenteuil and Louveciennes.

Flood at Port Marly, Sisley

- His depictions of the Seine in flood and the snowbound suburbs of Paris constitute 'pure' Impressionism.

Impressionist years

- Sisley exhibited seven paintings in the first Impressionist exhibition of 1874 and although Monet's influence was quite evident, he did not attract the same scornful criticism as the others.
- He continued to exhibit with them and for the third Impressionist exhibition of 1877 he presented the remarkable series of paintings showing villages overrun by floods.
- These paintings show a peaceful image of nature and many consider them his finest paintings.

Impressionist exhibitions

- Between 1874 and 1886, the Impressionists had eight exhibitions in Paris and one in New York.
- These exhibitions varied quite a bit.
- The art collector Paul Durand Ruel supported the artists but the period after the Franco-Prussian war was a difficult time in which to buy and sell art.
- Ruel's support gave the Impressionists the confidence to mount an independent exhibition.

The Anonymous Society of Artists

- The group chose 'The Anonymous Society of Artists' as the title for their first exhibition.
- The reviews were bad, the exhibition was badly attended and the artists suffered huge financial losses.
- However, the term 'Impressionism' had been established.

- Two years later they came together again but this exhibition was even less well attended. The reviews were no better.
- Edgar Degas was a member of the group but was dissatisfied with the name 'Impressionism' as well as with the predominant style of painting.
- Degas argued and disagreed with his colleagues a lot and eventually left the group.
- Over the years there were eight Impressionist exhibitions in Paris and a final one was held in America.

Impressionism in America

- The American artist Mary Cassatt was a substantial contributor to the last exhibition in Paris.
- Her American contacts were vital in helping Durand Ruel organise a huge exhibition in New York in 1886.
- American buyers brought the long-awaited financial success to the artists.
- By this time, all members of the group had gone their separate ways.

Edgar Degas (1834–1917)

- Hilaire Germain Edgar Degas came from an aristocratic family background.
- He took part in most of the Impressionist exhibitions and was one of its most important members.
- His work and awkward personality set him apart from the other painters.
- He disliked the word 'Impressionist', preferring to call himself a 'Realist' or 'Independent'.
- He also tried to capture fleeting moments in time but disliked outdoor or *plein air* painting.
- He admired the solid traditions of the old masters but his own paintings featured scenes of modern life: racecourses, theatres and cafés.
- He is most famous for his countless images of dancers.
- He visited the Paris Opera and sketched performances of the ballet. He focused on the dancers' gestures and poses as they practised, waited and stretched in the rehearsal room.
- Later in his career he painted controversial scenes of women bathing.
- Degas became interested in Japanese prints and this led him to experiment with unusual angles. His subjects are often cropped at the edges.
- Degas enjoyed spending hours talking about art in the Café Dubois with Édouard Manet and the other young artists, but he had an aloof manner and sharp tongue.
- He had very few close friends and apparently no love affairs. He was intensely private, particularly about his studio.
- Degas worked in a wide range of media, including oil, watercolour, chalk, pastel, pencil, etching and photography.

Horses

- Degas drew and painted all kinds of horses, including racehorses and scenes from the racetrack.
- Horseracing clubs in Paris were based on the British model and were very exclusive.
- Both Manet and Degas had friends among the upper classes who frequented these clubs.
- The newly developed racetrack of Le Longchamp was one of the fashionable sites in Paris.
- Degas set many of his paintings at Longchamps, including *At the Races, Gentlemen Jockeys* and *Jockeys in front of the Grandstands.* In these paintings, Degas has used space very cleverly to convey an image of swiftness.

Café scenes

- The cafe was the meeting place of Parisian society.
- Both Degas and Manet painted scenes in cafés.
- Beer had become a popular drink and Manet included this in several of his cafe pictures.
- Degas depicts a woman in a café but the atmosphere he creates could not be more different from that of Manet.

Absinthe

- The scene in this Degas painting seems to reflect nineteenth-century public concern about alcoholism and in particular the increase in women's drinking.
- The light in the café suggests morning and the woman sits with shoulders slumped, a glass of absinthe in front of her.
- Her legs are splayed out, eyes cast down and she has an expression of hopelessness on her face.
- The man next to her appears to be drinking cold black coffee, probably to relieve a hangover.

Absinthe, Degas

Le Café-Concert des Ambassadeurs

- Cafés often had huge stages and hosted outdoor café-concerts.
- Degas produced many pastels and prints based on the female performers at these concerts.
- *Le Café-Concert des Ambassadeurs* was a famous café on the Champs-Élysées.
- Gas lighting came before electricity and can seen in the globes behind the figure and the footlights that light up the performers.
- This creates unusual shadows and flesh tones but heightens the vibrant red of the dress.

The Opera

- Female dancers became Degas's favourite theme and he produced a huge number of paintings and pastel drawings on paper over his career.
- He spent a good deal of time observing the dancers' movements at the Opera and then brought the dancers to his studio.
- Here he made drawings and paintings of performance on stage, groups at rehearsal resting or waiting to perform.
- He also had a model spiral staircase, which can be seen in his paintings.

The Rehearsal

- This is a superb example of Degas' early work.
- Figures are crowded into the upper left and lower right, separated by a large area of floor space.
- A spiral staircase forms a very striking rhythm on the left.
- The dancers against the light of the window are contrasted by the dancer resting in the foreground with the blue-green shawl set off against the reds of the girl and her mother next her.

The Dancing Class

- This is one of Degas' most famous ballet pictures. It was shown at the first Impressionist exhibition of 1874.
- It is a complex arrangement of dancers and their mothers in groups on three sides of the famous teacher Jules Perrot. Perrot was a famous male dancer in his youth.
- In a typical Degas gesture, the dancer seated on the piano scratches her back.
- Another twists her earring as she reads.
- At their feet near the piano is a watering-can used to keep the floor boards moist and a little dog, who presumably accompanies one of the mothers.

The Dancing Class, Degas

- At the rear, dancers relax in different poses with their mothers. One is seated, wrapped in a red shawl, while another stands with arms around her daughter, as though consoling her.

Mothers and daughters

- Apprentices began official ballet classes at age seven or eight and studied long hours, without pay, for several years.
- They had to pass several important exams in stages, by which time they could earn more money than their fathers.
- Mothers looked after their daughters during these times and Degas regularly included them in his pictures.

Pastel drawings

- Degas produced many of his drawings in pastel, especially when his eyesight deteriorated.
- Often, he dampened the surface of the paper to achieve the effect he wanted.
- In *L'Etoile*, the viewer is seated in one of the boxes overlooking the stage and has an uninterrupted view of the dancer making her entrance salute. Degas has included one of the men who spent time backstage with the dancers.

Carriage at the Races

- Degas painted people he knew by placing them in a setting typical of them. He rarely charged for these portraits.
- Paul Valpinçon was his best friend from school and they remained close throughout their lives. He painted his friend and his family sitting in their carriage on a day's outing in *Carriage at the Races*.
- The focus of the picture is the baby with his nurse.
- The mother, bending under a parasol, and the father, dressed in the formal clothes of wealthy Parisians, gaze at their son.
- Even the father's dog seems to follow his gaze.

The Orchestra of the Opéra

- Another friend of Degas was Désiré Dihau, the bassoon player in the orchestra of the Paris Opera.
- Degas chose to depict him during a performance but changed the position normally occupied by such a musician. He is placed instead at the front centre.
- This was the first time Degas painted the ballet dancers for which he became so famous.
- The brightest area of the dance is immediately above Mr Dihau and the deepest bend of a dancing leg perfectly imitates the angle of his bassoon.

The Orchestra of the Opéra, Degas

Post-Impressionism

- In the late 1880s, a group of young painters broke away from Impressionism.
- Each abandoned naturalism in favour of their own highly personal art that expressed emotions rather than simply visual impressions. Some concentrated on themes of deeper symbolism.

exam focus

Make sure you understand the influence of artistic movements like the Impressionists and Post-Impressionists on later artists. Learn to discuss this and make comparisons in your answers.

- These artists are today called Post-Impressionists, but for the most part they worked independently and did not view themselves as part of a collective movement.
- The term 'Post-Impressionists' was first used by the British art critic Roger Fry in 1910.
- He organised an exhibition in London that year with the title 'Manet and the Post-Impressionists'.
- The artists included Paul Cézanne, Paul Gauguin, Vincent van Gogh and Georges Seurat.
- These Post-Impressionist artists influenced generations of artists to follow and their work laid the foundation for some of the major movements of early twentieth century: Expressionism, Cubism and Fauvism.

Neo-Impressionism

- At the last Impressionist exhibition in 1886 Georges Seurat exhibited a huge painting called *Sunday Afternoon on the Island of the Grande Jatte*.
- It was the main attraction of the show and stunned the Parisian art world.
- Using colour theory in a completely different way the young artist challenged the accepted Impressionist style.
- His technique, based on points of pure colour, was known as Neo-Impressionism.
- The method involved placing hundreds of small touches of complementary colours together to capture the effect of colour and light in a 'scientific' way.
- Using small dots or points of colour, which gave rise to the name 'Pointillism', the colours combined before the spectator's eyes in an optical illusion but remained glowing and light.
- It was immediately recognized as a new direction for modern painting.
- This systematic, logical approach to the style did not last very long.

Pointillism

- 'Scientific Impressionism', 'Divisionism' or 'Pointillism' was now attracting the attention of the press.
- The art critic Félix Fénéon was particularly impressed and his articles created tension between the Neo-Impressionists and Claude Monet's ideas.
- Fénéon first used the term 'Neo-Impressionism' and described it as a 'conscious and scientific' approach towards the problems of colour and light.
- According to Feneon: 'Seurat's divisionist art was superior to Impressionism and the most innovative style of the day'.

Georges Seurat (1859–1891)

- After his studies at the École des Beaux Arts, Georges Seurat became deeply interested in scientific theories on colour and vision.
- He spent two years devoting himself to black and white drawing.

Bathing at Asnières

- Seurat's first huge canvas showed people swimming and relaxing on the riverbank at the popular bathing place of Asnières.
- The painting was refused by the Salon, so Seurat and several other artists founded the Societé des Artistes Independants.
- They held an exhibition that was unsuccessful but here Seurat met Paul Signac a younger, largely self-taught painter.
- Seurat's next painting was once again set near Asnières.

Bathing at Asnières, Seurat

Sunday Afternoon on the Island of the Grand Jatte

- Seurat travelled to this spot every day, sketching all morning before returning to the studio where he painted in the afternoons. The giant canvas took two years to complete.
- The colours were spectacularly bright. The natural colours of objects mingled with complementary colours: red with green, and orange with blue.
- This changed the objects and gave the effect of reflected sunlight.

Sunday Afternoon on the Island of the Grande Jatte, Seurat

- It is more formal-looking than Impressionism and has a timeless and somewhat mysterious quality.

Paul Signac (1863–1935)

- Paul Signac was strongly influenced by Impressionism. He became enthusiastically involved with the small group of artists and the theories of Pointillism or Divisionism.
- He was a keen sailor and his paintings are mainly seascapes from Le Havre to Marseilles, Collioure, St-Tropez and even Venice.
- He had a more outgoing personality than Seurat and his enthusiasm was of immense benefit to him.
- Georges Seurat died at the age of 31. Signac became the leader of the Neo-Impressionists, but without Seurat the movement came to an end.

Paul Cézanne (1839–1906)

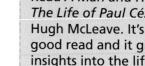

- Paul Cézanne was one of the most influential artists in twentieth-century painting.
- He inspired generations of modern artists but it was many years before his genius was appreciated.
- His achievements in painting were recognised only in the later years of his life. By that time rejection and ridicule had made him an embittered recluse.

> **key point**
>
> Read *A Man and His Mountain: The Life of Paul Cézanne* by Hugh McLeave. It's a really good read and it gives valuable insights into the life and work of the painter.

Links with Impressionism

- Cézanne came from Aix-en-Provence in the south of France.
- He came to Paris to study and it was here that he came in contact with the Impressionists and Pissarro.
- He moved in the same circles as the Impressionists and exhibited at some of their shows.
- He was first introduced to Manet, Degas and their friends at the Café Guerbois by Pissarro. However, he was never really an Impressionist and he had a vision in art beyond that of anyone working around him.
- He was known as a difficult character and his early paintings were of quite morbid subjects.

Influence of Pissarro

- The real strength in his work appeared only when he began to work with Pissarro.
- He settled at Auvers-sur-Oise, a village in the countryside near Paris, in 1872.
- He listened to Pissarro's advice and the two artists worked side-by-side out of doors.
- Pissarro's emphasis on meticulous observation of nature influenced Cézanne's work in a profound way. It led to a transformation in his painting.

Aix-en-Provence

- Cézanne had always admired the great masters from the past and had constantly struggled to make his painting 'solid and enduring like the art in the museums'.
- He was critical of the Impressionist artists' obsession with colour and light. He thought this would lead to a collapse of structure and that the paintings would eventually be no more than a brightly coloured, blurred haze.
- Eventually he returned to his native town of Aix-en-Provence. He felt he could achieve his aims only by working with nature at its clearest in the dry, transparent air.
- His father had been wealthy and Cézanne inherited his estate, so he was free from financial worry.
- He remained in Aix and painted the surrounding landscape until his death in 1906.

Struggles in painting

- Cézanne's work is strikingly original but throughout his career he battled with contradictory forces that caused his painting to be slow and painful.
- He wanted to go beyond what he considered the disorderly aspect of Impressionism in capturing the fleeting moment, yet he still wished to preserve the freshness of nature evident in Impressionist painting.

Cezanne's subjects

- Cézanne painted the landscape around Aix and Marseilles, but he also worked in his studio.
- For him the subject itself was of little or no importance. He preferred to work with inanimate objects, such as pieces of fruit, because they did not move or talk.
- He ignored the texture or the flavour and concentrated only on the colour and shape.
- He began to push forms towards geometric shapes. He famously remarked that painters should 'treat nature as a cylinder, sphere or cone'.
- Gradually his work became more about organising shapes and colours with an emphasis on structure and composition. He also adjusted the rules of perspective to suit the composition.
- Cézanne painted nudes but the flesh did not interest him. He used the bodies only to build up the structure in his painting.

Portraits

- Cézanne painted portraits of his wife and son, along with several self-portraits.
- He also painted some of the workers on the estate, but these paintings convey very little feeling about the character of his sitter.
- In many ways his portraits have the same qualities as a still life. They are solemn but almost majestic; it is their quiet appearance and grave colours make them very moving.
- Cézanne tried to paint the art dealer Ambroise Vollard. He sat for over a hundred sittings but Cézanne eventually abandoned this work and said he was only satisfied with the front of the shirt.

Mont St Victoire

- Cézanne's favourite landscape subject was Mont St Victoire; he painted over sixty versions of the mountain.
- In the early paintings the mountain is often framed by trees. He painted from more or less the same viewpoint, but it gradually loomed nearer and larger in his pictures of later years.
- Later versions are painted with greater freedom but still emphasize the solidity of the subject. However, the structure seems less obvious without the emphasis on lines.

Signed paintings

- Cézanne was rarely satisfied with his work. He signed only those paintings that he was completely happy with.
- When he died many paintings were found rolled up in his studio. These had failed to meet the exacting standards he had set for himself.

Still Life with Apples and Oranges

- This painting emphasises many points of vision at one time.
- Perspective has been adjusted to tilt the table forward in the interests of composition.
- The fruit, table and chair are shown from different viewpoints to emphasise the structure and form.
- The fruit, painted in vibrant glowing colour, spills from the plate onto folds of white cloth.

Still Life with Apples and Oranges,
Cézanne

- The carved wooden chair and velvet cushion are particularly richly depicted.
- The whole composition is set against a background of loudly patterned cloth, painted with dramatic energy in its deep twists and folds.

The Card Players

- The rich yellows and greens of the jackets, the orange of the table and the green of the bottle contrast with the white cards.
- Both men are depicted quite realistically and have a sculptural, three-dimensional quality.
- The table is slightly tilted up and the legs appear to be seen from several different viewpoints.

Le Mont St Victoire

- The strong and permanent shape of this solid limestone mass rising out of the surrounding countryside continued to fascinate Cézanne from the 1870s to his death.
- He concentrated on a strong pattern of brushstrokes, using dense and vibrant blocks of colour to build up the structure of the mountain, sky and houses in the foreground.

Le Mont St Victoire, Cézanne

- In these later versions, the brushstrokes are arranged in slabs of vibrant colour, forming an almost abstract composition.
- In every painting, the mountain retains its form and sense of grandeur.

The forerunner of Modern Art

- Cézanne recognised that he was responsible for the beginning of a new era in art. He said: 'I have blazed a trail; others will follow.'
- Others did follow: he inspired many of the vital movements of the first half of the twentieth century.
- While he is considered the forerunner of modern art, his body of work amounts to much more than mere trendsetting. His painting is the result of an individual struggle, rather than being part of an intellectual movement.
- This gives Cézanne's work its strength and makes it unlikely to ever fall out of favour.

Paul Gauguin (1848–1903)

- Paul Gauguin was a well-to-do stockbroker with a wife and five children.
- He spent his childhood in Peru and began painting in 1873, when he was working in Paris.
- As an amateur 'Sunday painter', he had come in contact with Corot and spent many weekends painting in the countryside.

Links with the Impressionists

- In 1877 he met with Pissarro and became involved with the Impressionists.
- This was to be a turning point in his life and for the next six years or so he spent his holidays working with Pissarro at Pontoise.
- Under the influence of Pissarro he turned to bright primary colours. Years later, Gauguin (who was not always generous to his fellow artists) admitted that Pissarro was the master from whom he had learned a great deal.
- Gauguin exhibited with the Impressionists at five of their shows, but the Impressionist artists were not all accepting of him.
- Monet and Renoir in particular disapproved of their shows being open to 'any dauber' but Degas seems to have admired Gauguin's work and even bought some of it.
- Gauguin's membership in the group was tolerated because of his friendship with Pissarro and also perhaps because of his wealth.
- He built up quite a collection of Impressionist paintings and particularly admired the work of Degas and Cézanne, in spite of Cézanne's acute dislike of him.
- In 1883 he resigned his job and took his family to his wife's home in Copenhagen.
- He later returned to Paris and his painting career began to advance.

Pont Aven

- In 1886 Gauguin made his first visit to Pont Aven in Brittany, where he gathered a considerable following about him and was at last in the role of a master.

- Pont Aven was for him an escape from Paris and civilisation. He felt that the rural life was making him young again.
- In 1888 he spent some time with Van Gogh in the south of France at Arles.
- This period turned out to be disastrous for both artists and Gauguin returned to Paris.
- Gauguin was now becoming well known and his painting had acquired a new and personal stamp thanks to the influence of Japanese prints and the work of Cézanne.
- Gauguin felt that it was important not to paint too closely from nature but to draw it out, to dream about it and think more of the creation that resulted from this.
- He reduced his shapes to flat areas surrounded by strong outlines and used only the most dominating of nature's colours.
- Gauguin more or less did away with shadows, made very little use of linear perspective and suggested depth in his pictures mainly through blocking planes of colour.

Tahiti

- In the end, a desire for a more primitive life led him to travel to Tahiti. His finest work was produced here.
- He used the Tahitian people to work through the mystery of human existence, which fascinated him.
- His paintings have an exotic character that is never simply picturesque, but expresses deep feelings.
- He regarded the primitive life with nostalgia but was always aware that he could never be innocent enough to become part of this 'lost paradise'.
- This accounts for a an element of melancholy in his work and strange titles, such as *Where do we come from? Who are we? Where are we going to?*
- His dealer in France, Ambroise Vollard, sent him a regular allowance. However, buyers proved unreliable and he fell deeply into debt.
- He was constantly in trouble with the colonial authorities and his life in Tahiti was in many ways more difficult than his time in France.
- Amazingly, none of this turbulence shows in his cool, timeless and mysterious paintings.
- He was sentenced to jail for three months for libel but while on appeal he died suddenly of a heart attack in May 1903.

Bonjour Monsieur Gauguin

- Set in Brittany, this painting takes its name from a painting by Courbet that Gauguin had seen a year earlier in Montpellier.
- Gauguin uses the title to symbolize the depression he was feeling about his artistic life.

Two Women on a Beach

- This was painted in 1891, shortly after Gauguin's arrival in Tahiti.
- It depicts two Tahitian women on the beach and shows the bold colour and design that Gauguin discovered in primitive art, with its flat forms and vibrant colours.
- Gauguin presented a view of the island of Tahiti as a serene and peaceful haven.

Two Women on a Beach, Gauguin

- In reality, this Tahiti had long since disappeared; but the vision of a gentle, content, primitive society was readily accepted in France when his work was shown there after his death.

Tahitian Girls with Mango Blossoms

- The women of Tahiti, with their gentle, classic beauty, fascinated Gauguin and he painted them many times.
- This painting is one of the most beautiful of his Tahitian works.
- Dressed in South Sea Island costume, they represent Gauguin's dream of an idyllic society.
- The women carry a basket of mango blossoms, the most typical flower of the tropics. It seems to represent an offering of their innocence and purity of spirit.

Where do we come from? Who are we? Where are we going to?

Tahitian Girls with Mango Blossoms, Gauguin

- This was painted at a time of deep depression for the artist.
- His health was by now ruined by alcohol and syphilis, his daughter in Denmark had just died and he had huge financial worries.
- After he completed the huge canvas, he even attempted suicide by taking arsenic.
- The tree and two figures suggest the tree of good and evil in the Garden of Eden. The reference to the Garden of Eden points to Gauguin's hopes to find paradise in Tahiti.
- The central figure stretches to pick the fruit from the tree, symbolizing the pleasures of life.
- Behind her is the dark figure of an idol with arms outstretched; this is a reminder of the menace that always lurks around humanity.

Influence on Picasso

- After Gauguin's death, an exhibition was held in the first Salon d'Automne in Paris in 1903. Another major retrospective in 1906 had a powerful influence on the French avant-garde (new and experimental artists) and in particular on Pablo Picasso.
- Picasso made paintings of oversized nude women and these monumental sculptural figures were directly influenced by the work of Paul Gauguin.
- Gauguin's work led directly to Picasso's landmark painting of 1907: *Les Demoiselles d'Avignon*.

Vincent van Gogh (1853–90)

- Van Gogh's painting career was one of the shortest but most intense in the history of art.
- He died at thirty-seven years of age, only four years after he discovered his style and eight years after he began painting.
- He was brought up in rural Holland as the son of a Dutch minister and took up painting only after various failures in his life had driven him to despair.
- He was deeply affected by all the poverty around him and wanted to be a preacher.
- His personality was not suited to this, but it was a severe blow to him when his licence to preach was withdrawn.

Painting

- Art soon became van Gogh's mission.
- His first paintings were of peasants and they show a deep concern and respect for the working life and its hardships.
- These early pictures are coarsely rendered and painted with rugged brushstrokes in dark, earthy tones.
- He came to Paris in 1885 and saw the final Impressionist show.
- He met Pissarro, who explained the Impressionist techniques to him. Later he met Paul Gauguin, whom he admired intensely and with whom he shared a love of strong colour and the linear strength of Japanese prints.
- Under Gauguin's influence, van Gogh's painting lost its heaviness and sentimentality.
- His colours were transformed and his brushstrokes broken into fragments.
- He painted still life paintings, views of Paris and portraits, but he found life in Paris frustrating.
- His intense and highly-charged, nervous personality became restless. We can see this from his self-portraits of the time.
- These early portraits were quite Impressionist, in technique, but in mood they point the way to more Expressionist work.

Arles and the South

- Van Gogh went to the south of France, settling in Arles in the region of Provence.
- The architecture, landscape and people fed his imagination. Influenced by Japanese prints, he was thrilled with the sun and its brightness and saw it as 'being as beautiful as Japan'.
- He worked at a frenzied pace but his brushstrokes broadened, his drawing became more confident and his colours stronger and brighter.
- He was supported mainly by an allowance from his brother Theo, to whom he wrote regularly, outlining his struggles with his painting and sharing his thoughts.
- He tried to express emotion, so he exaggerated what he considered important and dismissed that which he considered trivial or insignificant.

Gauguin

- Van Gogh dreamed of starting an artists' colony in Arles and begged Gauguin to join him.
- Van Gogh's brother Theo encouraged him to share his rented house and gave him money to furnish it.
- The house was painted in his favourite colour, yellow, which delighted him.
- In the 'Yellow House' he created a series of paintings of his room, hoping to impress Gauguin.
- However, Gauguin's stay was a disaster and the artists quarrelled badly.
- In one of these quarrels, van Gogh attacked Gauguin and later that evening cut off a piece of his own ear.
- Gauguin left and van Gogh suffered an increasing amount of breakdowns.

The Asylum in St-Rémy

- The people of his locality regarded van Gogh as a dangerous lunatic and he signed himself into a mental asylum at St-Rémy, a town near Arles, in April 1899.
- He spent one year there but it proved to be one the most creative times in his life as an artist.
- He painted the garden of the hospital and its flowers: irises and lilacs.
- He also painted the nearby landscape, producing some of his most enduring images, such as *Starry Night*.

Auvers and Dr Gachet

- Van Gogh later moved back to Paris, where he settled in a café at Auvers under the watchful eye of Dr Gachet, a friend and patron of the arts.
- Van Gogh worked as intensely as ever. While his colours were less brilliant, his canvases were filled with wild swirling lines.
- In spite of a black despair that overcame him, his painting remained full of vigour, control and careful composition.

- In his paintings, yellow cornfields wave and swell under a cloud of crows and trees, weaving dramatically into whirling skies of intense sun, moon or stars.
- Eventually van Gogh lost the battle with depression and on 27 July 1890 he shot himself in a cornfield while working at his easel.
- He died two days later, attended by his brother Theo and Dr Gachet.

Self-Portrait

- Van Gogh wrote that the best way to improve as a painter was to study the human figure.
- He was unable to afford a model, so he frequently painted self-portraits.
- There are thirty-five self-portraits in existence.
- The artist's tortured personality can clearly be charted in these intensely honest self-examinations.

Self-Portrait, van Gogh

Van Gogh's Room

- *Van Gogh's Room* is painted in the simplest manner, with pure colour and strongly outlined shapes.
- He painted two of everything: two pictures on the wall, two pillows on the bed, and two chairs to celebrate the arrival of a friend at the end of his months of solitude.
- The colours are a harmony of yellows, browns and pale blue.

Van Gogh's Room, van Gogh

Starry Night

- Painted at the St-Rémy asylum in June 1889, the painting shows Van Gogh's private world of symbols.
- The sun appears as a friendly element but the moon and the stars represent the turbulent forces of the night that threaten the peaceful life of the village.
- The stars grow ever larger in the swirling sky and seem destined to crash into the earth.
- He includes a cypress tree, characteristic of Provence and the rocky landscape of the countryside of St-Rémy.

Starry Night, van Gogh

Influence on Matisse and German Expressionism

- Van Gogh became one of the most admired of all modern masters but he sold only one painting in his lifetime.
- His Expressionist technique strongly influenced Henri Matisse (1869–1954) and his circle of Fauvist painters, as well as the German Expressionists.

2005 Ordinary Level paper: Section II, Question 11

Vincent van Gogh (1853–90) painted *Crows in the Wheatfield*, which is illustrated below. Answer (a), (b) and (c).

(a) How does van Gogh create atmosphere in this painting?

(b) Name and describe another painting by van Gogh, giving two reasons why you find this work interesting.

(c) Give a short background to Van Gogh.

Use sketches to illustrate your answer.

2005 Higher Level paper: Section I, Question 14

Discuss the innovations in painting that developed in the second half of the nineteenth century.

Support your discussion with reference to named works by at least two artists.

Illustrate your answer.

2006 Higher Level paper: Section I, Question 15

The Impressionists were celebrated for their depiction of light and everyday life.

Discuss this statement with reference to two Impressionist artists and give a detailed account of one painting of an outdoor scene by each.

Illustrate your answer.

2007 Higher Level paper: Section I, Question 14

Cézanne, Gauguin and van Gogh, often referred to as Post-Impressionists, were important influences on the art of the twentieth century. Discuss the contribution of these artists to the development of modern art referring to at least one painting by each artist.

Illustrate your answer.

2008 Higher Level paper: Section I, Question 13

His unique style and choice of subject matter set Edgar Degas (1834–1917) apart from other artists of the nineteenth century.

Discuss this statement with detailed reference to any one of his works.

and

Compare briefly your chosen work by Degas with a named painting by another nineteenth-century artist.

Illustrate your answer.

SAMPLE EXAM QUESTION

The work of Monet (1840–1926) and Renoir (1841–1919) epitomised the visual characteristics of Impressionism.

Discuss this statement making detailed reference to one painting by each artist.

Illustrate your answer.

Always introduce your answer. For this question, give a very brief account of Impressionism. Mention the aims and influences of the group and introduce both artists before going on to fully expand your points.

SAMPLE ANSWER

Impressionism was a major movement in art in France during the late nineteenth and early twentieth centuries. It began when a group of young artists rejected the Academic system then in place and set out to explore quite a different approach to painting. They painted out of doors and their main aim was to accurately record the transient effects of light on colour.

They became known as Impressionists after a newspaper critic saw a painting by Claude Monet called *Impression Sunrise* and described the paintings as mere sketches or impressions.

The most influential member and leader of the movement was Claude Monet and his work more than any other epitomises the visual characteristics of Impressionism. This can be seen quite clearly in his painting *Woman with a Parasol*.

Woman with a Parasol

The Impressionists discarded the idea of using paid models. Rather than using hired models to pose, Monet preferred to use friends. In the case of *Woman with a Parasol*, he used his wife Camille as a model. He painted the same subject several times but in this particular version he included his son Jean. He captured the atmosphere of a family outing, rather than an artificial scene where the models are posing. Madame Monet and the child are clearly painted in movement, walking in a field casually.

Woman with a Parasol is a fantastic piece that shows it was painted outdoors. The movement of *en plein air* is a key characteristic of Impressionism within this painting. The thick brush strokes suggest that the painting was done quickly to capture the fleeting moment. It also creates the feeling of a breeze around Camille and we can see the wind whipping past her and through the field due to the artist's distinctive brush strokes. The setting itself, true to *en plein air*, is a field. Monet chose to paint in the great outdoors rather than inside a studio. Because this painting is done outdoors, the light is more natural and authentic than the forced and unnatural light provided in a studio.

Monet was greatly influenced by an earlier artist Camille Corot. He worked for some time with Corot and other artists who had chosen to work outdoors, beginning what became known as the *en plein air* movement. This idea of a snapshot or fleeting moment in time with a landscape setting and figures greatly inspired Monet.

Photography

Another influence on Monet was the rising popularity of photography. This can be observed in *Woman with a Parasol.* The angle at which this painting is done resembles a photo taken by a camera. The figures are being viewed from an angle, looking up at them rather than on even ground. The shadows on the field intensify the contrast between that of the fields and the blue sky with white clouds. There are brushstrokes of green for the field, white for the wind, and a clear blue sky in the background. Camille Monet is the main solid figure connecting these elements. The horizon line creates a sort of optical illusion with the help of the intense colours. When the field reaches the sky, the horizon is given a dead-end effect. This creates a sense that Madame Monet is balancing on a tightrope with her parasol, much like a tightrope artist performing a balancing act with umbrellas in a circus. This 'line' is clearer as the green field comes to a sudden halt immediately where the blue sky begins.

Luncheon of the Boating Party

Monet has been called the Father of Impressionism, but another of the great Impressionist artists was Pierre Auguste Renoir. He worked closely with Claude Monet and his paintings include a wide range of Impressionist traits, such as *en plein air* scenes of everyday life, landscapes, and visible brushstrokes that capture a fleeting moment in time. Like Monet, he placed complementary colours side-by-side on the canvas, allowing the law of optics to create 'optical mixing' or the mixture of colour to form in the spectator's own vision. Renoir's work features lots of feathery brushstrokes but great solidity when it comes to figures. He loved pretty woman and included many in contemporary clothing in his work. All of these characteristics can be seen in *Luncheon of the Boating Party*.

The colours in *Luncheon of the Boating Party* include blue dresses, blue hats, yellow straw hats and a red marquee above. These colours create optical mixing within the painting. The atmosphere of a social scene is created within the activity in the painting. We see many different levels of activity in the foreground: a woman plays with a dog; three people talk casually, their colourful clothing adding to the optical mixing with a white vest, yellow hat and blue dress on display; and the wine bottles are studies in still life painting. In the middle ground more people casually enjoy the party: the man in the brown suit draws our eye straight to the centre of the painting; while the pair of men talking in the background also command our attention. Soft brushstrokes are seen in the greenery; this, as well as the soft blue colouring, contributes to the Impressionistic subject matter of landscape.

Composition

If we look closely, we see four females carefully placed throughout the painting: two in the foreground and two in the background. Each woman is facing in the direction of the painter/viewer. These four women in composition create a triangle. Because they appear composed, facing the painter and are painted with such solidity, we see the care with which Renoir treats the female human figure. In this delightful scene of modern middle class life, the sun filters through the orange striped awning and everything is bathed in its warm light; the women's faces in particular seem to glow.

> **key point**
>
> Learn to adapt your exam answers! The section on *Luncheon of the Boating Party* above could be used again in your answers to the two questions from the 2009 paper listed below. It could form part of your essay on Renoir or it could be used for 'a painting depicting a meal'. You might compare it to *Dejeuner sur l'Herbe* by Édouard Manet.

All of the crucial characteristics of Impressionist painting are present in Monet's *Woman with a Parasol* and Renoir's *Luncheon of the Boating Party*, from *en plein air* to modern subject matters. In this way both artists truly epitomised the visual characteristics of Impressionism in their work.

Donal de Bhá, 2009

2009 Higher Level paper: Section I, Question 13

Auguste Renoir (1841–1919) was a leading artist of the Impressionist movement. Name and discuss a figurative painting by Renoir, referring to subject matter, composition and the treatment of light on the figures.

and

Give a brief account of three characteristics of Impressionist painting.

Use sketches to illustrate your answer

SAMPLE EXAM QUESTION

Answer (a), (b) and (c)

(a) Choose and name a work that fits into one of the following categories:

- A painting depicting a meal
- A self-portrait of an artist
- A painting that depicts war
- A painting that features children
- A work by Damien Hirst.

> **key point**
>
> If a question asks you to contrast, make sure you choose relevant points. In the following question it is important to study both paintings and describe the areas that can be contrasted. The use of headings will often make an essay clearer, easier to read and even easier to write.

(b) Discuss the work you have chosen in detail, making reference to style, composition/design, technique, the artist and the period in which it was produced.

(c) Name and briefly discuss one other example from the same category.

Use sketches to illustrate your answer.

SAMPLE EXAM QUESTION

Describe and discuss the subject matter and imagery of *Luncheon of the Boating Party* by Pierre Auguste Renoir (1841–1919) and *Sunday Afternoon on the Island of the Grande Jatte* by Georges Seurat (1859–1891).

Refer in your answer to colour, composition and to the treatment of light and the human figure.

SAMPLE ANSWER

Pierre Auguste Renoir, born in 1841, was one of the most important artists in the Impressionist movement. Working closely with his friend Claude Monet, he was very influenced by this artist, known as the Father of Impressionism. Working together outdoors or *en plein air*, they painted everyday scenes of people enjoying social outings. In an effort to capture the effect of light, particularly on water, they used loose brushwork and large dabs of pure colour to suggest a fleeting moment in time. This 'optical mixing' allowed the colours to blend in the spectator's own eye. For a while the work of Monet and Renoir was so alike it was difficult to tell them apart, but while Renoir tended to use feathery brushstrokes his work also showed great solidity when it came to figures. Monet continued to paint landscapes, but Renoir preferred the human figure and in particular pretty women in contemporary clothing. This is seen very clearly in his painting, *Luncheon of the Boating Party*.

Pointillism

Luncheon of the Boating Party contrasts greatly with *Sunday Afternoon on the Island of the Grande Jatte* by Georges Seurat. Seurat, born 1859, founded a movement that challenged Impressionism. It was called the Divisionism or Pointillism movement. The huge painting *Sunday Afternoon on the Island of the Grande Jatte* caused a sensation when it was exhibited at one of the Impressionist exhibitions. It was the main attraction of the show and it stunned the Parisian art world. The term 'Neo-Impressionism' was used for the first time. Although Seurat continued the Impressionist idea of painting landscape and social scenes out of doors, he had gone beyond Impressionism to a more 'scientific and conscious' approach.

Colour theory

Inspired by the latest findings of a scientist called Ogden N. Rood, Seurat used colour theory in a completely different way. Instead of the loose brushstrokes favoured by the Impressionists, he used hundreds of dots of pure complementary colours side-by-side. These combined before the spectator's eyes in an optical illusion to capture the effect of colour and light. It was immediately recognised as a new direction for modern painting. It moved away from the Impressionists' effort to capture the essence of a fleeting moment in time.

Party atmosphere

In Renoir's *Luncheon of the Boating Party* the optical mixing of colour is created by loose and feathery brushstrokes. This is seen in the blues of the dresses and hats, as well as the yellow straw hats and red marquee above. All colours add to the atmosphere of this social scene. The 'party' is created with the many goings-on in the painting. In the foreground we see: a woman playing with a dog; three people casually talking; and still life studies of wine bottles. In the middle ground more people casually enjoy the party; the man in the brown suit draws our eye straight to the centre. The pair of men talking in the background also gain our notice. The green of the landscape and the soft blue sky remind us that this is very much still an Impressionist painting.

Composition

Composition also plays a very important role this Renoir painting. Looking closely, we see that the four females are carefully placed: two in the foreground and two in the background. Each woman is facing in the direction of the painter/viewer. These four women in composition create a triangle. Because these women appear composed, facing the painter and are painted with such solidity, we see that Renoir treats the female human figure with a great deal of care.

The Human Figure in *Sunday Afternoon on the Island of the Grande Jatte*

In contrast with Renoir, Georges Seurat does not have an interest in the solidarity of the human figure. This is an everyday scene of contemporary Parisians, but there is no sense of a naturalistic portrayal of real people. Many of the faces are not clear and there is no sense of movement or interaction amongst any of the groups or individuals. Instead the painting is focused on the science of colour.

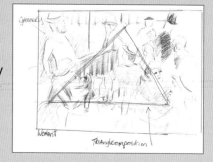

Composition

Seurat totally rejected the arbitrary nature of Impressionism in his building up of this complex, monumental composition. In the foreground to the right, three people are seen casually sitting down. A man with a pipe, a woman with a book and a moustached man with a cane and top hat are quite clearly together and yet they appear psychologically isolated. The wet nurse, wearing an orange headscarf, is reduced to a geometric shape. In the foreground to the left, we see the separate classes of people—lower, middle and upper class—relaxing alongside each other. In reality such a group would never have existed in that society. To the right we have a fashionable couple. In the centre middle ground, a woman is holding a small child. These three groups isolated from one another create a composition. The eye is therefore immediately drawn to the young girl in white.

Bright colours

The colours in *Sunday Afternoon on the Island of the Grande Jatte* are spectacularly bright. Natural colours of objects mingle with complementary colours: red with green, and orange with blue. This changes the colours completely and succeeds in creating the effect of reflected sunlight. The overall effect is more formal-looking than Impressionism and it holds a timeless and mysterious quality. Although the light is very bright, the shadows come to an immediate dead end in a sharp cut-off point. Seurat's systematic, logical approach did not last very long and the short-lived movement of Pointillism ended soon after the artist's death at the early age of thirty-one.

Daniel Waugh, 2010

SAMPLE EXAM QUESTION

Write as fully as you can on one of the following artworks:

The Deposition of Christ by Giotto (1266–1337)

The Birth of Venus by Sandro Botticelli (1446–1510)

The Mona Lisa by Leonardo da Vinci (1452–1519)

The Haywain by John Constable (1776–1837)

Two Ballet Dancers in a Dressing Room by Edgar Degas (1834–1917)

Starry Night by Vincent van Gogh (1853–90)

exam focus

In a straightforward question like the one below, make sure to fully discuss the given painting. Once again it is very important not to give irrelevant information that will gain no marks whatsoever! Remember: this question does not ask you to tell all you know about van Gogh and his work.

Describe your chosen work, referring to its subject matter, composition and colour. Give some general information about the artist and briefly discuss one other example of his work.

Use sketches to illustrate your answer.

SAMPLE ANSWER

Painted during a period spent in the asylum in St-Rémy, van Gogh's *Starry Night* is a masterful work of Expressionism. The stars explode like fireworks in a dark night sky that pulsates like an immense wave of energy. The forceful brushstrokes show a frenzied animation brought to life and encapsulated within. This shows van Gogh's expression and epitomises his distinct use of colour and unique style.

Born in Holland, Vincent van Gogh first came to Paris in 1885, where he met some of the Impressionists. He left Paris after a short time and travelled south to Arles in Provence where he was captivated by the light and the colours. Working at a frenzied pace, his strokes broadened, his drawing became more confident and his colours became stronger and brighter. He now applied colours in dashes and thick impasto swirls that stood out from the canvas.

Letters to Theo

Van Gogh always had tremendous support from his younger brother Theo, who helped him in every possible way both emotionally and financially so that he could devote himself to his painting. Vincent wrote numerous letters to Theo, pouring out his feelings about his life and work. He told his brother that he was not satisfied to paint just what he saw. Instead he tried to express emotion using pure colour. He exaggerated what he considered important and dismissed that which he considered trivial or insignificant. He used contrasting colours like red and green as he tried to express human passion.

Mental problems

Throughout his life, van Gogh had suffered from mental problems and this became much worse in later years. He signed himself into the asylum at St-Rémy and from here he continued painting with a furious intensity, producing numerous works in a very short time. Van Gogh was greatly inspired by the rocky landscape in the countryside around St-Rémy and the little village actually resembled a Dutch village with its distinctive church spire.

Starry Night

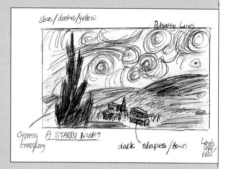

In his painting *Starry Night* he includes a cypress tree, so characteristic of Provence. Flaring upwards on the left, it cuts through all grounds–foreground, middle ground and background. The direction of this tree is in total contrast with the direction of the immense swirl seen in the sky. The brushstrokes are different also: on the tree we see long strokes but in the sky the stars are painted briskly with dashes. The tree seems to mimic the tower of the church in the centre middle ground. Van Gogh includes dark outlines around the distant buildings but the bright yellow of the swirling stars against the vibrant dark blue of the sky suggest deep emotion and may be an insight into van Gogh's damaged psyche.

Armchair

Another work of art by Vincent van Gogh was his simple piece entitled *Armchair*. This simple artwork shows a chair. A candle is perched on top and it emits an eerie glow, illuminating the piece. However, the colours, both pure and contrasting, show Expressionist qualities. The chair is painted blue, red and green with hints of yellow from the candle also. Like *Starry Night*, this chair is outlined in black, emphasising the solidity of its shape and the contrasting bold colours. This is a very distinct style from Vincent van Gogh and it had never been used by the Impressionists that came before him.

The subject matter is not a strong element here. Van Gogh was more concerned with applying his Expressionistic methods to still life and in my opinion he does so very well. The lit candle contrasts well with the blue, green and red. It may express anger, depression or a combination of emotions.

Van Gogh was to greatly influence modern art and his distinctive style and use of bold and vibrant colours paved the way for the art movement called Expressionism. Inspired by van Gogh, artists used colour to express emotion in painting. Unfortunately though, the artist who became one of the most admired of all modern masters had a short and sad life. He sold just one painting in his entire life and by the age of thirty-seven he was suffering from deep depression. In the end, one day while he was painting in a cornfield, he shot himself with a revolver and died a few days later.

Daniel Waugh, 2009

SAMPLE EXAM QUESTION

Cézanne, Gauguin and van Gogh, often referred to as Post-Impressionists, were important influences on the art of the twentieth-century. Discuss the contribution of these artists to the development of modern art, referring to at least one painting by each artist.

Illustrate your answer.

TIPS FOR YOUR ANSWER

- You can use some of the material from the sample answer on van Gogh (above) to answer this question.
- Note that the three artists mentioned worked quite separately, although they have been categorised as Post-Impressionists.
- Therefore your essay could be composed of three very distinct sections. Just ensure that you open with one paragraph relating to all three artists and that you end the essay in a similar way.

Twentieth-century art movements
Fauvism

- At the beginning of the twentieth century, a group of artists turned the order of French painting on its head.
- At an exhibition in Paris called Salon d'Automne (Autumn Salon) in 1905, the French public were presented with glaring reds, startling blue outlines and purple shadows.
- This was perceived as something of an attack on the senses.
- One art critic selected a piece by Matisse and said it was a 'Donatello among the wild beasts (*Fauves*)'. After that, the artists became known as *les Fauves*.

Colour

- Fauvism was not an art movement as such and the group had no theory or strong philosophical ideas.
- Colour bound them together, as did the vision of Henri Matisse and the landscapes of the south of France.

The Artists

- The main influence on the group was Gauguin, but the artists' approach varied quite considerably.
- Maurice de Vlaminck was deeply impressed by van Gogh and painted in strong bright colours, particularly red.
- André Derain used pure colour outlining, as Gauguin had done, in blue. He sectioned the colours into separate compartments in a method known as *cloisonnisme*.

Unusual colour harmonies

- The Fauves looked for unusual colour harmonies and rejected the traditional method of light and shade in favour of shapes constructed only with line and colour.
- Painting for them was first and foremost a flat surface to be covered with colours assembled in a certain order.
- Colours were not just for decorative purposes. Like van Gogh and Gauguin, the Fauves felt that colour should bring out feelings and sensations.

The end of Fauvism

- The movement lasted three years only.
- It came to an abrupt end when Henri Matisse became dissatisfied with its crudeness and lack of discipline.
- In 1908 the artists went their separate ways and Matisse embarked on a highly productive career.
- This was to earn him a revered place in twentieth-century art history, second only to Picasso, his great rival artist.

Henri Matisse (1869–1954)

- Matisse was a master of colour and he constantly explored its potential.
- He was also captivated by the sculpture of Africa and Islamic art.
- He developed a style characterised by vivid colour and bold patterns in his own expression of an ideal world.

Influences

- Matisse was introduced to the work of the Impressionists and van Gogh early in his career, but Cézanne's work had the greatest impression on him.
- In the midst of mounting misfortune and continuous derision from critics (and even his own father) Henri Matisse came close to abandoning painting for good.
- However, he weathered each storm and kept creating new works, all of which he chose to paint with his distinct modernistic approach.
- After the exhibition of 1905 the group acquired the title *Les Fauves* but Matisse never liked this.
- He was acutely aware of the complex problems produced by the movement and knew that random application of bright colours was not the essential point.
- His aim was to prove that colour did not need modelling, perspective or the traditional light and shade.
- He argued that pure colour could create volume and space that would not take away from the richness of the picture.

The South

- The south of France was a source of great inspiration to Matisse. In 1905 he went to Collioure to work with André Derain.
- He developed the strong and vibrant tones of colour that were to shock the viewers of the Autumn exhibition.
- Matisse used his wife as his model but these paintings caused a particular furore.
- Matisse was taken aback by this hostility but came to accept that any publicity was welcome.

Pattern

- Matisse loved pattern in all kinds of fabrics and had a particular liking for Islamic art after he saw an exhibition in Munich in 1910.
- The human figure is not permitted in Islamic art. Matisse was intrigued by the use of elaborate patterns instead.
- Matisse lived through some of the greatest changes and turmoil of European history, but none of this is reflected in any way in his painting.

Hotel windows

- In 1917 he moved more or less permanently to the south of France to an apartment in the Hotel Regina situated above the town of Nice.
- Here he painted many scenes through the window: the wrought-iron balcony, the shutters, the curtains, the chair and always the strip of blue Mediterranean sea.
- All of these works from the hotel window share a theme: a sense of the outside world as seen from a position of comfort and security.

A successful career

- Matisse became very successful in the 1930s and received large commissions to paint murals for American millionaire Dr Barnes.
- In 1941, after an operation for cancer, he was confined to a wheelchair.
- He continued to expand his work and experimented more with line drawing, illustrating poems.

The Chapel at Vence

- One of the highest points of his career was the commission for the Chapel of the Rosary in Vence.
- In gratitude to the nuns who had nursed him through his illness, he created all the wall decorations, the stations of the cross, furniture, stained-glass windows, even the vestments and altar cloths.

Cut-out shapes

- In his last years he relied greatly on cut-out shapes, which he applied directly onto the canvas or pinned to the wall.
- These simple bright colours recalled the simplicity and joy of childhood imagination.
- Matisse acquired fame and fortune in his lifetime.
- His work was shown in a large retrospective exhibition in the Museum of Modern Art in New York in 1951.
- He died in 1954.

The Green Line

- The model is Matisse's wife Amelie and the painting was shown at the Autumn exhibition of 1905.
- Matisse bypassed the traditional method of light and shade and replaced it with areas of flat colour in strong contrasting tones.
- Viewers at the Autumn Exhibition found the use of strong unnatural colours difficult to accept in the human figure.
- They were shocked to see a portrait in such startling colours with a huge green stripe running down the face of the model.

Henri Matisse, *The Green Line (Portrait of Madame Matisse)*, 1905; oil on canvas, 40.50 cm × 32.5 cm (15.9 in × 12.8 in). Statens Museum for Kunst, Copenhagen, © Succession H. Matisse / DACS 2011

Woman with a Hat

- Matisse's wife also posed for this painting.
- Painted in loud contrasting colours she wears a huge, gaudily-decorated hat and holds a fan.
- Critics were shocked by the artist's undisciplined and bold style in general, but *Woman with a Hat* was singled out for particular attack.
- However, Matisse was very pleased when Leo Stein (brother to the avant-garde writer Gertrude Stein) bought the painting.
- The Stein family became very supportive of Matisse's work and introduced him to other influential art patrons.

Henri Matisse, *La chambre rouge (Red Room, Harmony in red)*, 1908/09; Oil on canvas, 180 × 220cm. Collection S. I. Schtschukin, Inv. No. 9660, St Petersburg, State Hermitage. Photo: akg-images, © Succession H. Matisse / DACS 2011

Harmony in Red

- Considered by many to be Matisse's masterpiece, the painting is dominated by the colour red.
- The table is covered in a decorative pattern, inspired by oriental art. It matches the pattern on the wall.

- The woman's black top and white skirt provides some contrast, as does the view from the window, which shows a green field, trees and bushes.

Cubism

- Cubism was one of the most influential art styles of the early twentieth century.
- It was created by Pablo Picasso and Georges Braque in Paris between 1907 and 1914.
- It left a lasting impression on the young artists working in Paris at the time and it laid the foundations of modern art.
- The word Cubism came about after a French art critic Louis Vauxcelles saw landscapes painted by Braque that had been influenced by Cézanne.
- Vauxcelles referred to the geometric forms in these abstract works as 'cubes'.
- Early Cubism was also linked to Primitivism and non-Western sources.
- Picasso's ground-breaking *Les Demoiselles d'Avignon*, painted in 1907, was also highly influential.
- The flattening-out of space and the breaking up of the shallow background in this painting became the characteristic features of Cubism.
- Picasso had first seen African art in 1907 in the ethnographic museum in Paris.

Georges Braque (1882–1963)

- Braque was a Fauve artist who changed direction.
- He greatly admired Cézanne and began by painting directly like him.
- He took solidity, which so obsessed Cézanne, even further.

Braque and Picasso

- In 1907 Braque began to work with Picasso and together they broke with the Renaissance system of perspective.
- They were influenced by Cézanne's manner of breaking space into interwoven planes of colour and they based their efforts on his famous remark that 'one must detect in nature the sphere, the cone and the cylinder'.
- They painted everyday objects like a bottle, glass, pipe, newspaper, guitar or violin.
- They fragmented them and brought them almost to the point where they no longer existed (in other words 'abstract art') but did not quite cross that threshold.
- They took the same approach towards the human figure.
- By painting things 'as one thinks them, not as one sees them' (Picasso), Cubism placed the thought process or 'conception' in artwork before imitation or the representation of reality.
- The work of art itself became a reality or a 'pictorial fact' (Braque). Painting became about itself and not what it represented.
- Braque adapted Picasso's manner of dislocating and Cézanne's innovations into the first easily recognisable Cubist paintings.

Reality in Cubism

- Cubism was never a rejection of reality.
- According to Cubist theory, a closer knowledge of nature required new methods of representing it.
- The artists' theory was that the eye is always moving and constantly changing, shifting its range of vision to reconstruct distances, surfaces and volumes.

Collage

- Picasso was the first artist to use collage or something other than paint on the surface of the canvas.
- In *Nature Morte à la Chaise Cannée* he used a piece of oilcloth to imitate the caning of a chair.
- Both Picasso and Braque continued to use paper, cloth and other textured materials in their paintings.

Violin and Pitcher: Braque

- The subject in this painting has been almost completely obscured.
- The volume of the objects are fragmented into separate components and then reassembled in a complex manner.
- The jug and violin can barely be detected in the shadowy surface.
- Tones of one colour create the effect of a soft, silvery, transparent light.

Pablo Picasso (1881–1973)

- For many people, Picasso is the artist who represents modern art.
- He was not in fact the most revolutionary artist of the twentieth century, but his name stood for everything that was daring, aggressive and extravagant.
- He turned convention upside down and bewildered the public with unexpected and sensational innovations.
- This earned him the reputation of an outrageous modern artist.

Blue Period

- Picasso first came to Paris in 1900 and within a year he was painting in cold blue tones.
- He painted young, sad, bloodless women, sickly children and old and emaciated beggars.

Rose Period

- Three years later he painted harlequins, acrobats and itinerant circus folk in pinks or 'rose' colours.
- The figures were still solemn and unsmiling, but not quite as mournful and depressed-looking as in the previous period.

Cubism

- In 1907 Picasso began to work with Georges Braque and developed the first ideas of Cubism.
- Cézanne influenced him considerably.
- He painted *Les Demoiselles d'Avignon*, one of the most powerful paintings of the century.
- This led the two artists to develop Cubism.
- During the years 1907 to 1914 Cubism went through several stages.
- Picasso and Braque worked closely together and for a while their work was almost indistinguishable from each other.
- Interestingly, Braque's artwork was always created in a slow and deliberate manner, while Picasso was always in a hurry.

Working alone

- After Braque was seriously wounded in the First World War, Picasso painted alone.
- In 1917 he went to Rome to design sets for the famous Russian Ballet company.
- He was introduced to a new and more glamorous social world.
- He married a dancer named Olga Khokova.
- He was inspired by his Italian experience to paint female nudes in the Neo-classical tradition of Ingres, the great nineteenth-century artist.
- These are large exaggerated figures painted in sombre tones of grey, grey-blue and pink.
- Picasso had not abandoned Cubist achievements; he simply alternated between the two styles.
- Between 1920 and 1924 Picasso painted his last Cubist works. Two great compositions from this time are entitled *Three Musicians*.
- Picasso's work changed as he searched continuously for a way to express himself with complete freedom.
- As an artist he watched the oncoming tide of the war in the 1930s with anguish.

The Spanish Civil War

- The Spanish Civil War greatly upset Picasso and the violence and emotion in his work reflected this.
- He painted several versions of *Weeping Women* as his homeland was torn apart by the war.
- The fate of the little Basque town of Guernica caused him to paint one of his most poignant works.

key point

General Franco, dictator of Spain, asked that *Guernica* should be exhibited in Spain. Picasso relentlessly refused and it remained in New York for many years as the centrepiece of the collection in the Museum of Modern Art. In accordance with Picasso's will, they reluctantly returned it to Spain in 1981, following that country's return to a democratic government.

- In one of the most brutal acts of war ever perpetrated, the town was razed by German Fascist bombers who were supporters of General Franco.
- Picasso painted this huge work in just over a month for the Spanish Pavilion in the 1937 World Fair.
- With its combination of Surrealist and Cubist imagery in figures and beasts it hit just the right note for the mood of the time.
- It touched people's consciences and was received with praise and unreserved enthusiasm, making Picasso a world famous artist.

South of France

- Picasso remained in Paris during the German occupation and then moved to the south of France.
- He remained here as a figure of huge popular acclaim with almost the stature of a film star.
- Until his death in 1973, Picasso painted, sculpted and experimented unceasingly.

Les Demoiselles d'Avignon

Les Demoiselles d'Avignon, Picasso

- This Picasso painting is considered the single most famous modern picture. It made Cubism possible.
- In an attempt to fuse several viewpoints at one time, the figures are stylised with limbs almost dislocated.
- The faces are distorted like African masks and the features are wrenched out of line with one another.
- The source for the strange faces of the women was Picasso's collection of African masks.
- The energy and distortion in African art greatly appealed to him.
- The picture also broke new ground in its brutal sexual frankness.
- The women are prostitutes on show and even now the distorted angles and eyes that stare straight at the viewer are disturbing.
- Picasso himself had a great fear of venereal disease and the painting seems to reflect this.
- There seems to be a threat in the women's stony gazes and even the melon in the foreground looks like a sharp weapon.

The Three Musicians

- The figures are all from the theatre and were inspired by his ballet, set and costume designs.
- The colours are flat and brilliant and feature one of Picasso's favourite figures, the harlequin.

- The monk sits on the right, Pierrot in his white costume in the centre and the harlequin on the left.
- The harlequin costume with its geometric possibilities fitted the style of Cubism perfectly.
- Picasso used it in many different styles of painting, including in a portrait of his son Paul.

Guernica

- The Spanish Civil War moved Picasso from his preoccupation with his own artistic and personal problems to depicting this terrible tragedy.

Guernica, Picasso

- Its message is a unique documentation of the horror and despair of the event.
- It is also the most powerful denunciation of the brutality of war ever depicted in modern art.
- The perpetrators of this violent act are not shown but their presence is everywhere.
- It is without doubt one of the milestones in twentieth-century art and it stands as a symbol of defenders of freedom against all forms of violence and tyranny.
- The media was always important to Picasso and the painting has the appearance of a screaming newspaper headline.
- He was undoubtedly affected by pictures in the London and Paris newspapers of the charred aftermath of the bombing and the eyewitness accounts from correspondents in Bilbao.
- The most important, largest and most expressive figure at the centre of the painting is the wounded horse.
- In contrast the bull expresses brute force.
- The five figures in the huge canvas express surprise, horror, grief, anger and despair.
- The fallen warrior lies between the horse's hooves. In his hand is a broken sword and a flower grows from his clenched fist.
- A woman throws her arms to the sky as she and the house are in flames.
- Another figure, reduced to the simplicity of a face and arm, stretches out of the window to light the scene with the lamp of freedom. She discovers with dazed horror the spectacle of death and destruction.
- A figure stumbles on her knees towards the screaming horse.
- At the side a woman raises her head to the sky and cries out in a scream of pain over the body of her dead child.
- She and the others seem to cry out not only for the tragedy of the town but in fear for all humanity.

2005 Ordinary Level paper: Section II, Question 13

Guernica is a famous work by Pablo Picasso (1881–1973).

Answer (a), (b) and (c).

(a) In your opinion what is this work about? Sketch **two** separate images from it to help you to explain your answer.

(b) Discuss this work under the following headings:

- composition
- technique.

(c) Name and describe one other work by Picasso.

Use sketches to illustrate your answer.

2005 Higher Level paper: Section I, Question 16

Answer (a) and (b).

(a) Describe and discuss the composition and art elements of *Harmony in Red* by Henri Matisse (1869–1954).

(b) Write an account of the Fauves and of the work of Matisse.

Illustrate your answer.

2006 Higher Level paper: Section I, Question 16

The artists who developed Cubism found new ways of depicting the world around them.

Discuss Cubism and explain how it was different from the art that had gone before.

and

Describe in detail one Cubist painting by Pablo Picasso (1881–1973) **or** Georges Braque (1882 –1963) and give your opinion of your chosen example.

Illustrate your answer.

2008 Higher Level paper: Section I, Question 15

The Old Guitarist, illustrated below, is typical of Pablo Picasso's (1881–1973) work from a particular period.

Describe and discuss *The Old Guitarist* in detail

and

Compare and contrast *The Old Guitarist* with another named work by Picasso from a different period of his artistic career.

Illustrate your answer.

SECTION 3

General Appreciation

- Topics vary considerably in this section of the exam, so it can be tricky to prepare for.
- Choose one or two areas of research from the list below.
- There is no guarantee that the topic you prepare will appear on the exam paper. Be flexible, be prepared to answer another question should this happen.
- If there is a study area of particular interest to you (e.g. film) then it is likely there will be a question to suit you on the exam paper.
- The original purpose of this section of the exam was to create an opportunity for you to discuss topics based on everyday visual experience in your own environment. You are not expected to be an expert in your chosen study area. Remember that in some general areas such as the environment, packaging, design, etc., your opinion is as good as the next. So be confident and express yourself well!

- To develop a critical awareness of a range of art works by visiting museums and galleries
- To develop a critical awareness of public art in Ireland by visiting and examining individual works
- To consider the relationship between public art and architecture
- To develop the skills to describe, discuss, analyse and contrast design of objects and architectural artefacts
- To develop confidence in individual preferences for differing styles and tastes
- To develop awareness of the aesthetic elements in film
- To read film reviews
- To have an awareness of film as a form of visual communication
- To acquire an understanding of filming techniques by researching a range of popular films in magazines or online

8 General Appreciation

Study areas

Museum and gallery studies

Gallery visits are fundamental to all aspects of the art syllabus. It is therefore vital to do the following:

- Visit an art gallery, art exhibition, museum or heritage centre.
- Read exhibition catalogues and other information relating to the visit.
- Find a website related to the gallery, museum or heritage centre.
- Examine the layout, lighting and labelling system of your chosen museum, gallery or heritage centre.
- Be informed about the history of the building and its location.
- Read reviews of exhibitions.
- Form your own opinions.

key point

A visit to a museum is the most common answer given. Therefore, yours needs to be special! Answer with enthusiasm. If you enjoyed the visit and found it special, then communicate that. If the visit helped your work in the classroom, explain this for the examiner.

Film studies

To broaden your understanding of this study area, it is crucial to:

- See lots and lots of films.
- Do some online research for background information on films.
- Watch the 'making of' features on DVDs.
- Research specific contemporary films.
- Research specific animated films.
- Gain knowledge of film-making techniques.
- Learn about animation techniques.
- Understand special effects.
- Study named film directors and their unique styles.
- Read reviews in newspapers and film magazines.

Local public sculpture

- Research public sculpture in your locality.
- Find out the name of the artist.
- Find further examples of this artist's work.
- Research examples of public sculpture in other localities.

- Examine sculptures on motorways and roads, as well as parks, streets and squares in towns and cities.
- Read reviews and media features on public sculptures.

The built environment

- Gain knowledge of architecture. Learn the names of new buildings and research the architects who designed them.
- Be aware of town planning: streets, squares, shopfronts, etc. Pay particular attention to new or redesigned towns.
- Examine the buildings and streets in your area and inform yourself of its history and design.
- Read newspaper or magazine articles on architecture and town planning.

Graphic design, interior design and product design

- General information and art terms from practical art class or home economics class may be useful to you here.

General topics

- Appreciation is intended to test a general knowledge of art and aesthetics, so why not try answering a very general question? Most exam papers will feature one such general question.
- For example, take the following question from the 2009 Higher Level paper. All that is required here is your opinion of somewhere quite familiar to you.

Pedestrianised areas have now become an attractive addition to the streetscape of many of our towns and cities.

Discuss this statement with reference to any specific example with which you are familiar. In your answer refer to lighting, paving, seating and planting

and

Discuss briefly your own ideas for a piece of public art that would enhance this area.

Use sketches to illustrate your answer.

TIPS FOR THE SAMPLE ANSWER

- Write an interesting, descriptive essay putting forward your own reasons as to why it is attractive.
- Address each of the specific elements listed in the question.
- Make your points with confidence, enthusiasm and even a bit of humour. Try to keep your examiner engaged!
- If you describe the area well and your ideas are good, you will pick up very easy marks.

- The design of the piece of sculpture is entirely up to you and involves mostly drawing. This makes it a lovely question for young artists. Go for it!

All of the following questions are open to individual opinion. Yours is just as interesting as the next. Use your everyday experience and studies in art to inform your answers.

SAMPLE EXAM QUESTIONS

(a)   Live theatre performance can be a stimulating visual experience, with its combination of set design and lighting, costumes and make-up, performance and sound.

Discuss this statement with reference to a performance you recently attended

and

Suggest a set design for any scene of your choice from a play you have studied for your Leaving Certificate.

Illustrate your answer.

(b)   Many shopfronts can be redesigned or restored, adding distinction to buildings and enhancing the overall character and attractiveness of our towns and villages.

Discuss this statement with reference to the illustration below

and

Outline your ideas and considerations that would enhance this shopfront.

Illustrate your answer.

(c)   Describe and discuss the magazine cover illustrated below, making reference to imagery, colour, typography and visual impact

and

Discuss briefly how computer editing can enhance photographic images for graphic design.

Illustrate your answer.

(d)   Product design involves a balance between appearance and function.

Discuss this statement with reference to any **two** of the following, referring to form, materials, function and decorative qualities.

- mobile phone
- electric kettle
- handbag or sports bag

and

Discuss briefly the influence of fashion trends on your chosen product over time.

Illustrate your answer.

A visit to an exhibition

This is one of the most popular questions on the
Appreciation section. This is very understandable because
in general a visit to a gallery and an art exhibition is a very
rewarding experience. Take the time on your visit to
examine the work, make notes and read reviews on the
newspapers or internet before and after. Take any
catalogues or leaflets that the gallery has to offer. If you enjoyed your visit, communicate
that in your answer. Be enthusiastic and don't be afraid to give your opinion!

key point

Do not make negative
comments about the work.
If you didn't like something,
simply leave it out!

exam Q

SAMPLE EXAM QUESTION

A visit to an exhibition is best judged by the quality of artwork on display and by
the gallery space itself.
Discuss this statement with reference to any named exhibition you have visited
and
Discuss two specific works from this exhibition in detail.
Use sketches to illustrate your answer.

SAMPLE ANSWER

An exhibition I visited was *Terror & Sublime: Art in an Age of Anxiety* at the
Crawford Gallery in Cork. This was held from November 2009 to February 2010
and featured a great variety of contemporary modern pieces from sculptures,
photography and projections, as well as a selection of biblical paintings dated
before 1900. This may seem a strange mix of past and present, but the themes
worked well in their separate galleries. All the works in the exhibition were
selected by the Curator/Director Peter Murray.

The exhibition was held in the Crawford's new wing galleries: two large rooms,
one above the other, connected by stairs. For me this space seemed perfectly
suited to the theme and added greatly to its impact.

The theme of the exhibition

The central message of the exhibition was that pronouncements of doom and
gloom are nothing new and it highlighted not so much the obstacles and
disasters facing humanity, but rather the capacity of people to survive adversity.

The distinct separation of a darkened ground-floor space and a brightly-lit upper
floor really made the atmosphere and added to the idea of *Terror & Sublime*. The
'terror' on the ground floor was set in very dim lighting and in that darkness the
eeriness was further accentuated by a strange gurgling sound coming from
American artist Jim Sanborn's *Critical Assembly*. This disturbing sculptural piece is
an artistic representation of the secret research for the first atomic bomb and it is
made of actual pieces of the electronic instruments and materials from the Los
Alamos Laboratory of the 1940s, 1950s and 1960s. Sanborn got these from
people in New Mexico who had worked on the Manhattan Project.

Spotlights placed above certain works added a glare and because the room was so dark sometimes they made it even more difficult to see clearly. The pictures were, however, all placed with great care and consideration, mainly at eye level.

Exhibit 1

One exhibit I found particularly interesting was Cecily Brennan's (born 1955) projection called *Unstrung*. It was two minutes on a 16 mm projector and was simply outstanding. The film showed a woman (Eimer O'Grady) standing in a white room gazing out. A sudden loud boom made me jump with fright as she was struck by a wave of oil. This was followed by a gushing sound and then as the waves ceased, she got to her feet, panting. Then she silently stared right at us. This deeply macabre contemporary horror film really affected me and seeing it in such a pitch black space added to the sense of terror. I feel the theme related to how Cecily Brennan herself feels as she is hit by the black oil of criticism. Two distinct subjects are clear here. The theme reflects psychological pain, affliction and trauma as well as the vulnerability of the human body and psyche. I really liked how this piece was totally different from any other exhibit at the exhibition. For me it was so true to the theme of *Terror and Sublime* with its terrifying and shocking images.

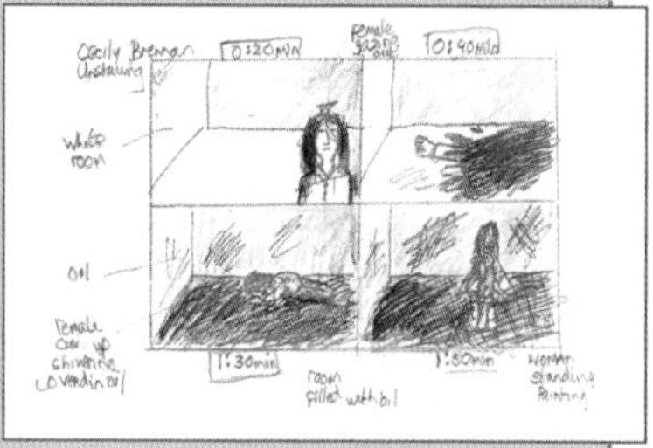

Upstairs, natural light poured through the large windows creating the 'sublime' and in complete contrast the paintings here were brighter and with rich blue colours. This included James Barry's *Portrait of Burke and Barry*, which hung at eye level.

Exhibit 2

A work that I really loved here was a photograph by Theresa Manigan called *Crone Forest*. The photographer used perspective effectively to show a downward shot of landscape and the figure sitting idly in the foreground to the left. This isolated character in a desolated barren forest showed the vulnerability of human beings in the face of nature, a theme that all of the works had in common. The bleak white and dull colours added to the emotive message of melancholy. I felt this image carried a hint of an influence by the modern climate crisis and was a way of expressing the artist's protest against

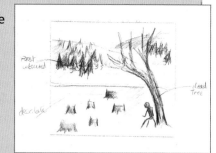

politics. This hope was a realistic and expressive one. I liked how there was no frame, as it would have taken away from the image.

Overall I really enjoyed the exhibition. The tour guide was very helpful and really made the exhibition exciting. The location of the Crawford Gallery is very well situated, in the heart of the city next to the new shopping quarter. Because of the free admission, I can visit future exhibitions. The contemporary macabre works were highly enjoyable and well worth a visit.

Daniel Waugh, 2010

SAMPLE EXAM QUESTION

Discuss how a visit to a gallery or museum impacted on your appreciation of art and how it influenced your own artwork.

Name the gallery or museum and refer to two specific examples of work in your discussion.

Illustrate your answer.

A question on a visit to an art gallery will sometimes give you an opportunity to discuss something special. See below how this student justifies her choice of a church as an art gallery.

SAMPLE ANSWER

Late last March some of my classmates and I were privileged enough to visit Paris on an art trip. We were unlucky that the Musee d'Orsay was undergoing renovation and we could not make an advance reservation for our group. But although we had to stand in the longest queue I have ever seen (almost two hours to get inside) I have to say I was not disappointed. Musee d'Orsay was buzzing with people of every nationality and filled with the most beautiful paintings. I was absolutely blown away by the room filled with Monet's paintings. Here one whole wall was filled with five paintings side-by-side of Rouen Cathedral. The paintings were completed by Monet at different times of the day in different lights. We also saw some large paintings he had made of his wife Camille standing in a windswept cornfield. These were especially interesting because just the day before we had visited the

Musée d'Orangerie to see the two magnificent oval rooms the artist had designed himself to display the huge canvases of the water lilies he had donated to the state.

Sainte Chapelle

Amazing as these museums were, nothing, and I mean nothing, could top the church we had seen earlier that morning: Sainte Chapelle, located in the centre of Paris. This is a church, a museum and most definitely an art gallery. It was the most amazing place I have ever visited. I never expected that I would like a church so much but it was the place I liked most on the art trip–even beating the magnificent Eiffel Tower! On entering I immediately decided I would get married there (if I ever won the Lotto).

The church is a little gem of Gothic architecture erected by Louis IX the King of France in 1248. I learnt about this in class but I must say it is so much more impressive in real life. The coloured roof with Islamic-like arches was gorgeous. The church is so colourful I'd never seen anything like it. What amazed me was this unusual combination of colours with the multi-coloured windows that should look so tacky, but don't.

The ceiling is held up with red pillars designed with gold illustrations. The roof itself is blue with red bordering and gold detail. The design on the roof was made to resemble 'star-filled heavens', which I think is a lovely idea. The vaults are then illustrated with *Fleur de Lys*, which with the contrasting stars, creates the alternation between royal and divine symbols. The church no longer holds mass or any services. What really annoyed me was that a stall selling souvenirs took up half of the downstairs area, covering stained-glass windows and sculpture. At first I refused to support them by boycotting their stalls but I ended up buying some over-priced postcards anyway!

Upstairs chapels

Upstairs is just as impressive: fifteen stained-glass windows consisting of 1,113 little pieces of glass dating mainly from the thirteenth century. How could you not love it? I was in awe of the height of the upstairs part; the glass alone is an amazing 15.4 m in length. These tall lancet windows form a wall of glass around the upper level and although they are all different colours, the predominant colours are red and blue. These blend together to give the whole area a purplish hue. The windows behind the main altar were unfortunately under renovation and covered with a cardboard photograph. This was a pity because this was where the light was shining in.

From my research I found out that the upstairs was designed so beautifully in order to house relics of the Crown of Thorns worn by Jesus when he was crucified. A beautiful rose window upstairs consists of blue, yellow, red, green, purple and pink. It really is outstanding. This however is not an original thirteenth-century piece; it was replaced in the sixteenth century. Its style is flamboyant Gothic. It shows an apocalypse around an enthroned Christ in the central oculus.

Influences

Visiting Sainte Chapelle greatly enhanced my appreciation of art. After the visit, I realised nothing compares to this church! I had never taken notice of the stained-glass windows or sculpture in my own local church where I have been attending mass for the past twelve years of my life. Now I find myself sitting there, comparing and contrasting the design and art of my church with my beautiful Sainte Chapelle. The visit also improved my appreciation of architecture. It amazed me, especially the arches; I felt like I was in India.

The visit to the museums of Paris greatly helped my art. I love painting with acrylic and to see Monet's brushstrokes and Impressionist use of small dabs of colour to suggest light was very special. But still the most important visit was the one to Sainte Chapelle. The use of colour inspired me. I have always loved colour, but have been afraid to use it in my own work in case it looked childish or tacky. I will now be brave enough to use the kinds of colour and ornate patterns that I saw on the statues of the saints standing around the walls upstairs in Sainte Chapelle. Sainte Chapelle is an amazing church and art gallery and I will definitely be back after the renovations.

SAMPLE EXAM QUESTION

Imagine you have been asked to show some visitors around a art gallery with which you are familiar. They have only a limited time but it is important that they leave with a good appreciation of the gallery's artistic merit.

What paintings in particular in the gallery would you choose to show them? Give reasons for your choices and describe these works in detail.

Illustrate your answer.

SAMPLE ANSWER

It would be difficult to leave Cork's Crawford Gallery without appreciating its artistic merit because, although it has a relatively small collection, it houses some superb paintings. Also the fact that the Gallery is quite small makes it easy to get around without getting exhausted and enables the visitor to see a considerable variety of work in a very short time. As well as paintings, the Gallery has another collection of very important works that I would first show my visitors because they are immediately inside the front door. A set of plaster casts was presented to Cork in the early nineteenth century and this marked the beginning of the art gallery. They are casts of classical Greek and Roman sculptures made by the sculptor Canova from originals in the Vatican Museum.

key point

This essay could apply to any gallery. The most important point is to put forward your own response to the work and a clear picture of gallery in question.

The Collection

The collection includes some of the most famous works from the Greek golden age, like the *Venus de Milo* or *Aphrodite and the Belvedere Torso*, which apparently Michelangelo used as a model for some of the figures in the Sistine Chapel. There is also the large complicated group of the *Laocoön* and his sons wrestling with the serpents. The originals in Rome are of course made of marble but I think the clean white plaster displayed against the deep red walls of the large gallery with natural lighting from the large roof window and its marvellous mosaic floor conveys their splendour exceptionally well.

The first one I would show my visitors is the Discus Thrower or *Discobolus* because it is my own favourite. This beautiful Greek athlete with his perfectly toned body would likely appeal to all who enjoy sport. It would remind them of the ancient Greek admiration not just for athletics but also for the human body.

Next we would go up the grand staircase with the wonderful stained-glass by Cork sculptor James Scanlon immediately facing us. Among its rich greens and blues is a tiny crack in the glass with a wry comment written beside it: 'but will the crack last?' Hopefully this should make everyone smile and examine the work a little more carefully.

Paintings

Finally I would bring them to the paintings in the main Gallery and the Crawford's most popular work: *Time Flies* by William Gerald Barry. This features an old woman leaning on her stick and some children playing on the bank of a

river in the trees. The landscape itself could be Fota, Co. Cork, where the artist grew up, but the church in the distance makes it more likely to be set in northern France, where he spent some time.

The title suggests the sadness of life passing, as the elderly woman watches over the carefree children. Oranges and browns conjure up a feeling of autumn as the surface of the river gleams in the background and even the shadows in the foreground seem to mark the passing of the day. The brightest light falls on the children, so the title could also be taken to mean 'time flies when you're having fun', with regard to the children playing. To me the painting feels like a captured memory, perhaps because of the late evening light spilling over the scene, or maybe because it reminds me of my own childhood. But then everyone remembers their own childhood, playing in the sun with someone watching over them, so I believe this painting would positively affect my visitors.

Men of the South by Sean Keating captures a singularly Irish moment. This large and very realistically portrayed painting shows six men in a 'flying column' waiting to begin an ambush. The arrangement of the five waiting men deliberately echoes an image of 'classical heroes' and the virtues of courage and resolve rather than the confusions and bloodshed of guerrilla war. The men are shown in profile holding their guns tense with eyes fixed in the same direction ready to ambush a passing military vehicle during Ireland's War of Independence. Painted in browns, greys and dark greens with the Irish countryside visible in the background, these are actual portraits of some of the revolutionaries made from sketches and photographs.

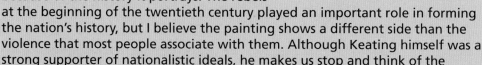

The reason I would choose this painting is because of the history it portrays. The rebels at the beginning of the twentieth century played an important role in forming the nation's history, but I believe the painting shows a different side than the violence that most people associate with them. Although Keating himself was a strong supporter of nationalistic ideals, he makes us stop and think of the individual characters and who they were as we examine them sitting on the hillside, resting yet ready to spring into action at any moment.

A *Portrait of William Orpen* by James Sinton Sleator is remarkable for its technique and attention to detail. The painting catches the eye because of its stark contrast between the sitter's white jacket and the dark background. A curtain included in the background also has the effect of adding depth to the work while pulling in the attention of the viewer. William Orpen was one of Ireland's foremost painters in the late 19th and early 20th century and his friendly expression as

he looks up from his own painting is so incredibly lifelike that one just has to linger a while and examine the work really closely to see how the artist achieved this. The tiniest of brushstrokes can be seen picking out the shine of the paints on the palette as well as the light and shadow on the artist's face.

As we leave I am hoping that my selection will have inspired my visitors to return to the gallery. I believe I would certainly have given them an appreciation of this small gallery's rich artistic worth, even in the short time allowed.

Caitriona Ahern, 2010

General Appreciation questions are not easy to prepare because they can vary greatly, but it is always worth looking over past questions. The question below presents you with a real opportunity to express something of great interest to yourself.

SAMPLE EXAM QUESTION

A recent book entitled *100 Everyday Marvels of Design* celebrates examples of great design.

Select any three everyday objects that you think should be recorded in such a book and give reasons for your choices. In your answer discuss suitability of design, function, form, materials and style.

Illustrate your answer.

SAMPLE ANSWER

Art is a very broad word. It can relate to a vivid image depicted on canvas or to a stone marvel chiselled from nothing. Everyday objects can also be works of art because of the clever design that is both aesthetically pleasing as well as functional. I would expect a book entitled *100 Everyday Marvels of Design* to include many objects that we see around us all the time and take for granted in this fast-paced world we live in. I would like to include in that book some objects that many young people use everyday, seldom appreciating their very special design. I will now draw attention to the design, function, form, materials and style of gaming controllers, guitars and finally glasses.

Examples

In the twenty-first century a new market has been opened up to the public: gaming. Prior to the twenty-first century there was a market for gaming (e.g. Super Nintendo, SNES, Sega Megadrive) and the control pads for these were either horrible, grotesque plastic squares with tiny inaccessible buttons or large oversized 1990s-style modern art controllers, which appalled the user. Until 'Next Generation Gaming' came along, two types of consoles dominated the market: Play Station (Sony) and X-Box (Microsoft). Each involved superb-looking modern machines that are practical and lightweight for travel. The PS3 Controller (as shown below) has a clear function: you push a designated button for a desired effect. Because of the well-designed buttons and layout, the desired function is easy to achieve. The control pad is designed to fit in the palm of your hand

with 100 per cent comfort. It is made of thick thermosetting plastic, which never changes shape, even under great pressure. The function that is most improved is the plug-in-and-play wireless function. Regardless of what console is being used, the operator can use a USB lead to plug in and play up to thirty hours of battery time. With a sleek, black look and a clear-glass coating, the style appeals to all. It could even be said that it has a futuristic look.

Guitar design

I believe that the twenty-first century saw a decline in entertaining music with the loss of one of the most stylish pieces of equipment known to man: the electric guitar. No single guitar is the same. Great companies like Fender, Gibson and EMP work tirelessly to give people stylish masterpieces such as Stratocastors, Les Pauls, Explorcers and Razorbacks. I wish to discuss a guitar called a 'V'. It gets its name from its shape (it is an upside-down letter 'v') and it is ideal for playing standing up or sitting down. The design comes in various forms depending on genre, from a 'King V' to a 'Flying V'. The 'Flying V' is a rounded finish with gloss paint. The design is optional, given the right amount of money! A 'Gibson Reverse V' is made with a solid mahogany body, ebony fretboard with a Gibson 57 Classic Pickups and a single volume knob. This leads to a modern curvy design. The function is how easy it is to pick up and play: you place your leg in the 'v' inlet and with cut-outs you can reach the lower number frets. It is a guitar used by many famous stars (including Dave Mustaine from Megadeth), so it deserves a place in *100 Everyday Marvels of Design*.

Everyday object

For my final choice of a completely everyday marvel of design, I would have to include something I heavily rely on. Without this object, I would be unable to enjoy any design at all: my glasses. These have been around since the eighth century when the Egyptians used the first magnifying reading glasses. The man who first claimed priority was Salvine Darmate of Italy in 1284.

In recent times people have lost their fear of having glasses. I know when I was young I didn't like wearing them as I was afraid of the ridicule. But with the cutting-edge science being used in the twenty-first century (even bringing back the Buddy Holly look), glasses are becoming a fashion accessory. Now the designs vary from thin to thick, black to white. Mine are thick and brown and well-designed. The function is obvious: glasses enable you to see. With a sturdy frame and a case for storage, glasses become rather practical. They come in a variety of styles from many different designers: Quicksilver, Roxy, Red or Dead, etc. Through this miracle of regained sight I can continue to appreciate the everyday marvels of design that the world has to offer.

Luke Murphy, 2009